MORE ABOUT BOY

Books by Roald Dahl

THE BFG
BOY: TALES OF CHILDHOOD
BOY *and* GOING SOLO
CHARLIE AND THE CHOCOLATE FACTORY
CHARLIE AND THE GREAT GLASS ELEVATOR
THE COMPLETE ADVENTURES OF CHARLIE AND MR WILLY WONKA
DANNY THE CHAMPION OF THE WORLD
THE ENORMOUS CROCODILE
ESIO TROT
FANTASTIC MR FOX
GEORGE'S MARVELLOUS MEDICINE
THE GIRAFFE AND THE PELLY AND ME
GOING SOLO
JAMES AND THE GIANT PEACH
MATILDA
THE MAGIC FINGER
THE TWITS
THE WITCHES

Picture books

DIRTY BEASTS
THE ENORMOUS CROCODILE
THE GIRAFFE AND THE PELLY AND ME
THE MINPINS
REVOLTING RHYMES

Plays

THE BFG: PLAYS FOR CHILDREN (*Adapted by David Wood*)
CHARLIE AND THE CHOCOLATE FACTORY: A PLAY (*Adapted by Richard George*)
DANNY THE CHAMPION OF THE WORLD: PLAYS FOR CHILDREN
(*Adapted by David Wood*)
FANTASTIC MR FOX: A PLAY (*Adapted by Sally Reid*)
JAMES AND THE GIANT PEACH: A PLAY (*Adapted by Richard George*)
THE TWITS: PLAYS FOR CHILDREN (*Adapted by David Wood*)
THE WITCHES: PLAYS FOR CHILDREN (*Adapted by David Wood*)

Teenage fiction

THE GREAT AUTOMATIC GRAMMATIZATOR AND OTHER STORIES
RHYME STEW
SKIN AND OTHER STORIES
THE VICAR OF NIBBLESWICKE
THE WONDERFUL STORY OF HENRY SUGAR AND SIX MORE

Collections

THE ROALD DAHL TREASURY
SONGS AND VERSE

ROALD DAHL

MORE ABOUT BOY

PUFFIN

PUFFIN BOOKS

UK | USA | Canada | Ireland | Australia
India | New Zealand | South Africa

Puffin Books is part of the Penguin Random House group of companies
whose addresses can be found at global.penguinrandomhouse.com.

puffinbooks.com

Boy first published in Great Britain by Jonathan Cape Ltd 1984
Published in the USA by Farrar, Straus & Giroux 1984
Published in Puffin Books 1986
Published as *More About Boy* with new material 2008
This edition published 2016
001

Set in Goudy Old Style
Printed and bound in China

A CIP catalogue record for this book is available from the British Library

ISBN: 978–0–141–36737–8

www.greenpenguin.co.uk

Penguin Random House is committed to a
sustainable future for our business, our readers
and our planet. This book is made from Forest
Stewardship Council® certified paper.

Contents

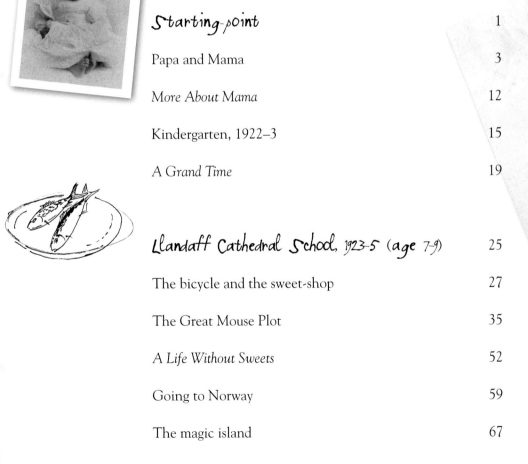

Even though I was born in the same street as Roald Dahl, I never knew him as a boy (however I was lucky enough to marry him years later, so mustn't grumble too much).

Although he told me a lot about his fantastical childhood, MORE ABOUT BOY has let me into some of the secrets he left out. My, what a story! Of course, it has all the familiar ingredients of growing-up, but it is also the tale of how so many of Roald's books came to be written. Look hard enough, and it's all there.

In 2005 – fifteen years after my husband died – the Roald Dahl Museum and Story Centre opened in his hometown of Great Missenden in England. The Museum is home to Roald's archive, full of all his jottings and scribbles and crossings out, as well as many of the letters and photos and school reports he mentioned in BOY. Much of this archive has never been seen before though, so it seemed a good idea to share a little of it with you now . . . which is why you are holding MORE ABOUT BOY. I do hope you enjoy reading – for the first time – about Joss Spivvis and the joys of Meccano and what happened next to the horrible Mrs Pratchett . . . I certainly did!

Felicity Dahl
Gipsy House
Great Missenden

For Alfhild, Else, Asta, Ellen and Louis

An autobiography is a book a person writes about his own life and it is usually full of all sorts of boring details.

This is not an autobiography. I would never write a history of myself. On the other hand, throughout my young days at school and just afterwards a number of things happened to me that I have never forgotten.

None of these things is important, but each of them made such a tremendous impression on me that I have never been able to get them out of my mind. Each of them, even after a lapse of fifty and sometimes sixty years, has remained seared on my memory.

I didn't have to search for any of them. All I had to do was skim them off the top of my consciousness and write them down.

Some are funny. Some are painful. Some are unpleasant. I suppose that is why I have always remembered them so vividly. All are true.

R. D.

Roald Dahl was sixty-eight when *Boy* was first published.

a letter from Papa

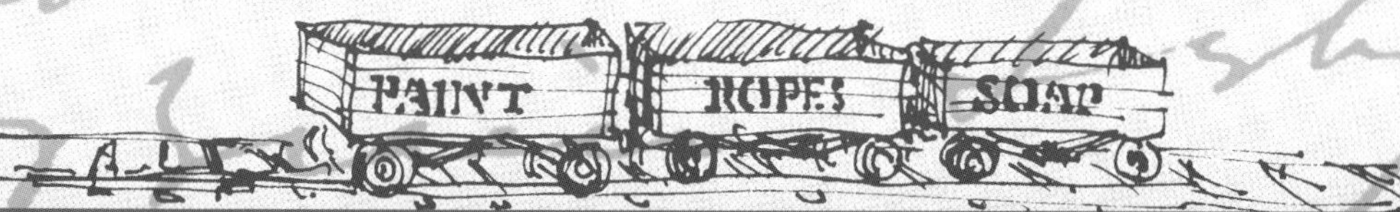
PAINT
ROPES
SOAP

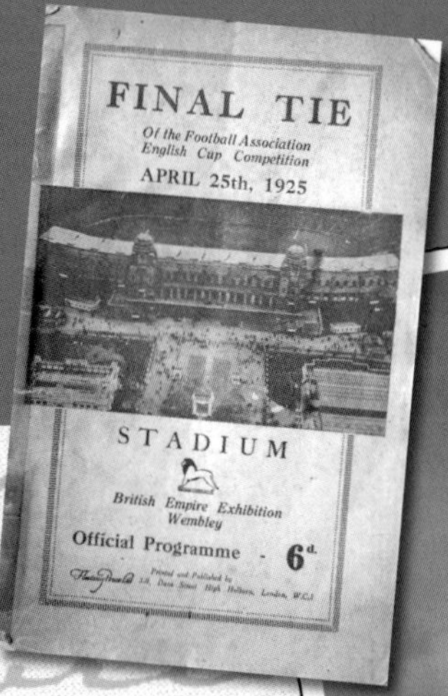
FINAL TIE
Of the Football Association English Cup Competition
APRIL 25th, 1925
STADIUM
British Empire Exhibition Wembley
Official Programme - 6d.

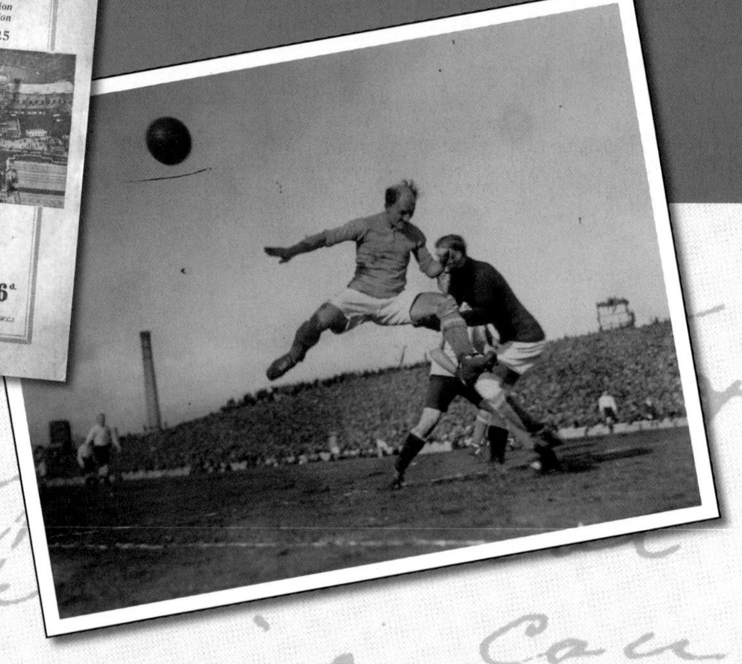

Starting-Point

THE COAL & SHIPPING EX_____
(CARDIFF) LIMITED.
1917.

No 3

PRINCIPAL MEMBER'S

Mr Harold Dahl

NOT TRANSFERABLE.

This Ticket is issued subject to the Rules and Regulations of the Exchange.

JOSEPH DAVIES & C. P. HAILEY,
Joint Secretaries.

This Ticket must be produced to the Commissionaires
whenever required.

E. W. Holder, Cardiff.

RD 20/6/1

TAFF VALE RAILWAY.

No. 3067   £ 5/3/11

M_r H. Dahl

Is entitled to travel by any of the Company's Trains
which are available for Ordinary Passengers

Between   Radur

and   Cardiff Docks

From   24 Oct 19 19

To   23 Apl 1920

inclusive

SUBJECT TO THE CONDITIONS ON OTHER SIDE.

Wendy House

Alfhild Ellen and Else me and Astri
Radyr

Papa and Mama

My father, Harald Dahl, was a Norwegian who came from a small town near Oslo, called Sarpsborg. His own father, my grandfather, was a fairly prosperous merchant who owned a store in Sarpsborg and traded in just about everything from cheese to chicken-wire.

I am writing these words in 1984, but this grandfather of mine was born, believe it or not, in 1820, shortly after Wellington had defeated Napoleon at Waterloo. If my grandfather had been alive today he would have been one hundred and sixty-four years old. My father would have been one hundred and twenty-one. Both my father and my grandfather were late starters so far as children were concerned.

When my father was fourteen, which is still more than one hundred years ago, he was up on the roof of the family house replacing some loose tiles when he slipped and fell. He broke his left arm below the elbow. Somebody ran to fetch the doctor, and half an hour later this gentleman made a majestic and drunken arrival in his horse-drawn buggy. He was so drunk that he mistook the fractured elbow for a dislocated shoulder.

'We'll soon put this back into place!' he cried out, and two men were called off the street to help with the pulling. They were instructed to hold my father by the waist while the doctor grabbed him by the wrist of the broken arm

Harald Dahl (1863–1920)

Roald Dahl's grandfather was Octovias Dahl. He and his wife Ellen had six children: three boys – Harald (Roald Dahl's father), Oscar and Truls; and three girls – Ragna, Olga and Clara.

3

and shouted, 'Pull, men, pull! Pull as hard as you can!'

The pain must have been excruciating. The victim screamed, and his mother, who was watching the performance in horror, shouted 'Stop!' But by then the pullers had done so much damage that a splinter of bone was sticking out through the skin of the forearm.

This was in 1877 and orthopaedic surgery was not what it is today. So they simply amputated the arm at the elbow, and for the rest of his life my father had to manage with one arm. Fortunately, it was the left arm that he lost and gradually, over the years, he taught himself to do more or less anything he wanted with just the four fingers and thumb of his right hand. He could tie a shoelace as quickly as you or me, and for cutting up the food on his plate, he sharpened the bottom edge of a fork so that it served as both knife and fork all in one. He kept his ingenious instrument in a slim leather case and carried it in his pocket wherever he went. The loss of an arm, he used to say, caused him only one serious inconvenience. He found it impossible to cut the top off a boiled egg.

'Amputation' comes from the Latin word 'amputare', meaning 'lop off'. Surgical amputations date back at least as far as the fourth century BC, and probably further. There were huge improvements in surgical techniques, anaesthetics and antiseptics before Harald Dahl was operated on. But it must still have hurt.

My father was a year or so older than his brother Oscar, but they were exceptionally close, and soon after they left school, they went for a long walk together to plan their future. They decided that a small town like Sarpsborg in a small country like

Norway was no place in which to make a fortune. So what they must do, they agreed, was go away to one of the big countries, either to England or France, where opportunities to make good would be boundless.

Their own father, an amiable giant nearly seven foot tall, lacked the drive and ambition of his sons, and he refused to support this tomfool idea. When he forbade them to go, they ran away from home, and somehow or other the two of them managed to work their way to France on a cargo ship.

To follow their journeys, have a look at the map on page 13.

From Calais they went to Paris, and in Paris they agreed to separate because each of them wished to be independent of the other. Uncle Oscar, for some reason, headed west for La Rochelle on the Atlantic coast, while my father remained in Paris for the time being.

The story of how these two brothers each started a totally separate business in different countries and how each of them made a fortune is interesting, but there is no time to tell it here except in the briefest manner.

Take my Uncle Oscar first. La Rochelle was then, and still is, a fishing port. By the time he was forty he had become the wealthiest man in town. He owned a fleet of trawlers called 'Pêcheurs d'Atlantique' and a large canning factory to can the sardines his trawlers brought in. He acquired a wife from a good family and a magnificent town house as well as a large château in the country. He became a collector of Louis XV furniture, good pictures and rare books, and all these beautiful things together with the two properties are still in the family. I have not seen the château in the country, but I was in the La Rochelle house a couple of years ago and it really is something. The furniture alone should be in a museum.

While Uncle Oscar was bustling around in La Rochelle, his one-armed brother Harald (my own father) was not sitting on his rump doing nothing. He had met in Paris another young Norwegian called Aadnesen and the two of them now decided to form a partnership and become shipbrokers. A shipbroker is a person who supplies a ship with everything it needs when it comes into port – fuel and food, ropes and paint, soap and towels, hammers and nails, and thousands of other tiddly little items. A shipbroker is a kind of enormous shopkeeper for ships, and by far the most important item he supplies to them is the fuel on which the ship's engines

Harald Dahl and Ludwig Aadnesen set up business in 1901 in Cardiff.

run. In those days fuel meant only one thing. It meant coal. There were no oil-burning motorships on the high seas at that time. All ships were steamships and these old steamers would take on hundreds and often thousands of tons of coal in one go. To the shipbrokers, coal was black gold.

My father and his new-found friend, Mr Aadnesen, understood all this very well. It made sense they told each other, to set up their shipbroking business in one of the great coaling ports of Europe. Which was it to be? The answer was simple. The greatest coaling port in the world at that time was Cardiff, in South Wales. So off to Cardiff they went, these two ambitious young men, carrying with them little or no luggage. But my father had something more delightful than luggage. He had a wife, a young French girl called Marie whom he had recently married in Paris.

In Cardiff, the shipbroking firm of 'Aadnesen & Dahl' was set up and a single room in Bute Street was rented as an office. From then on, we have what sounds like one of those exaggerated fairy-stories of success, but in reality it was the result of tremendous hard and brainy work by those two friends. Very soon 'Aadnesen & Dahl' had more business than the partners could handle alone. Larger office space was acquired and more staff were engaged. The real money then began rolling in. Within a few years, my father was able to buy a fine house in the village of Llandaff, just outside Cardiff, and there his wife Marie bore him two children, a girl and a boy. But tragically, she died after giving birth to the second child.

Harald Dahl married Marie in 1901 and they had two children: Ellen (born in 1903) and Louis (born in 1906). Marie died in 1907, aged twenty-nine. The family home in Fairwater Road, Llandaff was named 'Villa Marie' after her. (Roald Dahl was born here in 1916.)

When the shock and sorrow of her death had begun to subside a little, my father suddenly realized that his two small children ought at the very least to have a stepmother to care for them. What is more, he felt terribly lonely. It was quite obvious that he must try to find himself another wife. But this was easier said than done for a Norwegian living in South Wales who didn't know very many people. So he decided to take a holiday and travel back to his own country, Norway, and who knows, he might if he was lucky find himself a lovely new bride in his own country.

Over in Norway, during the summer of 1911, while taking a trip in a small coastal steamer in the Oslofjord, he met a young lady called Sofie Magdalene Hesselberg. Being a fellow who knew a good thing when he saw one, he proposed to her within a week and married her soon after that.

Mama Engaged

me at 8 months

Harald and Sophie's four children were called:

Astri (born in 1912),

Alfhild (1914),

Roald (13 September 1916)

and **Else** (1918).

Harald Dahl took his Norwegian wife on a honeymoon in Paris, and after that back to the house in Llandaff. The two of them were deeply in love and blissfully happy, and during the next six years she bore him four children, a girl, another girl, a boy (me) and a third girl. There were now six children in the family, two by my father's first wife and four by his second. A larger and grander house was needed and the money was there to buy it.

So in 1918, when I was two, we all moved into an imposing country mansion beside the village of Radyr, about eight miles west of Cardiff. I remember it as a mighty house with turrets on its roof and with majestic lawns and terraces all around it. There were many acres of farm and woodland, and a number of cottages for the staff. Very soon, the meadows were full of milking cows and the sties were full of pigs and the chicken-run was full of chickens. There were several massive shire-horses for pulling the ploughs and the hay-wagons, and there was a ploughman and a cowman and a couple of gardeners and all manner of servants in the house itself. Like his brother Oscar in La Rochelle, Harald Dahl had made it in no uncertain manner.

DAHL.—On the 13th inst., at Villa Marie, Llandaff, S. Wales, the wife of HAROLD DAHL—a son.

The big house at Radyr had the Welsh name 'Ty Mynydd' ('Tee Mun-uthe') which means 'Mountain House'. There were greenhouses, croquet lawns, gardens and pig sties!

the house at Radyr

But what interests me most of all about these two brothers, Harald and Oscar, is this. Although they came from a simple unsophisticated small-town family, both of them, quite independently of one another, developed a powerful interest in beautiful things. As soon as they could afford it, they began to fill their houses with lovely paintings and fine furniture. In addition to that, my father became an expert gardener and above all a collector of alpine plants. My mother used to tell me how the two of them would go on expeditions up into the mountains of Norway and how he would frighten her to death by climbing one-handed up steep cliff-faces to reach small alpine plants growing high up on some rocky ledge. He was also an accomplished wood-carver, and most of the mirror-frames in the house were his own work. So indeed was the entire mantelpiece around the fireplace in the living-room, a splendid design of fruit and foliage and intertwining branches carved in oak.

He was a tremendous diary-writer. I still have one of his many notebooks from the Great War of 1914–18. Every single day during those five war years he would write several pages of comment and observation about the events of the time. He wrote with a pen and although Norwegian was his mother-tongue, he always wrote his diaries in perfect English.

He harboured a curious theory about how to develop a sense of beauty in the minds of his children. Every time my mother became pregnant, he would wait until the last three months of her pregnancy and then he would announce to her that 'the glorious walks' must begin. These glorious walks consisted of him taking her to places of great beauty in the countryside and walking with her for about an hour each day so that she could absorb the splendour of the surroundings. His theory was that if the eye of a pregnant woman was constantly observing

HOW TO PRONOUNCE NORWEGIAN NAMES:

Sofie = So-fee-ah

Roald = Roo-arl

Astri = Os-tree

Alfhild = Olf-hill-d

Else = El-sa

the beauty of nature, this beauty would somehow become transmitted to the mind of the unborn baby within her womb and that baby would grow up to be a lover of beautiful things. This was the treatment that all of his children received before they were born.

Do you think Roald Dahl might have based the character of Danny's dad in *Danny the Champion of the World* on his own father?

'My father, without the slightest doubt, was the most marvellous and exciting father any boy ever had. Here is a picture of him.'

a letter from Papa

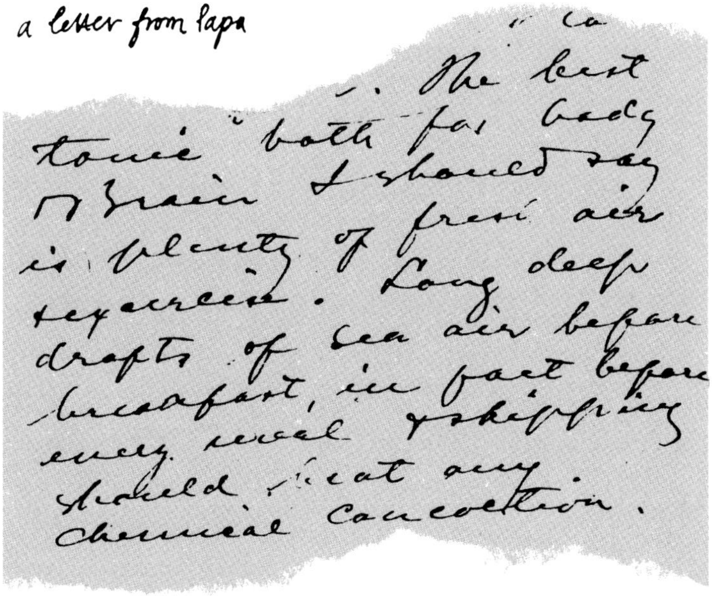
The best tonic both for body & brain I should say is plenty of fresh air & deep respiration. Long deep drafts of sea air before breakfast, in fact before every meal & skipping should beat any chemical concoction.

'You might think, if you didn't know him well, that he was a stern and serious man. He wasn't. He was actually a wildly funny person. What made him appear so serious was the fact that he never smiled with his mouth. He did it all with his eyes.'

More About Mama

Roald Dahl's mother.

She was undoubtedly the absolute primary influence on my own life. She had a crystal-clear intellect and a deep interest in almost everything under the sun, from horticulture to cooking to wine to literature to paintings to furniture to birds and dogs and other animals – in other words, in all the lovely things in the world. Her hair, when she let it down, as she did every morning so that she could brush it assiduously, reached three-quarters of the way down her back, and it was always carefully plaited and coiled in a bun on the top of her head.

My mother was widely read. She read the great Norwegian writers in their own language, Ibsen, Hamsun, Undsett and the rest of them, and in English she read the writers of her time, Galsworthy, Arnold Bennett, Kipling etc. When we were young, she told us stories about Norwegian trolls and all the other mythical Norwegian creatures that lived in the dark pine forests, for she was a great teller of tales. Her memory was prodigious and nothing that ever happened to her in her life was forgotten. Embarrassing moments, funny moments, desperate moments were all recounted in every detail and we would listen enthralled.

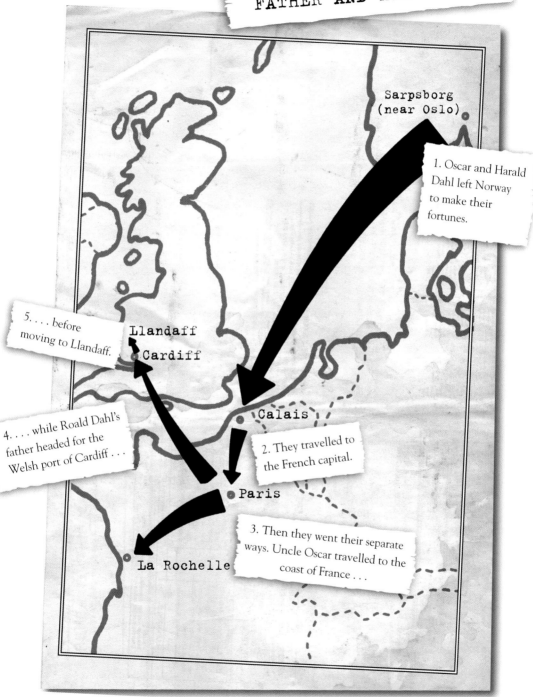

TRAVELS OF ROALD DAHL'S FATHER AND HIS UNCLE

Sarpsborg (near Oslo)

1. Oscar and Harald Dahl left Norway to make their fortunes.

Llandaff
Cardiff

5. . . . before moving to Llandaff.

Calais

4. . . . while Roald Dahl's father headed for the Welsh port of Cardiff . . .

2. They travelled to the French capital.

Paris

3. Then they went their separate ways. Uncle Oscar travelled to the coast of France . . .

La Rochelle

Kindergarten, 1922–3 (age 6–7)

In 1920, when I was still only three, my mother's eldest child, my own sister Astri, died from appendicitis. She was seven years old when she died, which was also the age of my own eldest daughter, Olivia, when she died from measles forty-two years later.

Astri was far and away my father's favourite. He adored her beyond measure and her sudden death left him literally speechless for days afterwards. He was so overwhelmed with grief that when he himself went down with pneumonia a month or so afterwards, he did not much care whether he lived or died.

If they had had penicillin in those days, neither appendicitis nor pneumonia would have been so much of a threat, but with no penicillin or any other magical antibiotic cures, pneumonia in particular was a very dangerous illness indeed. The pneumonia patient, on about the fourth or fifth day, would invariably reach what was known as 'the crisis'. The temperature soared and the pulse became rapid. The patient had to fight to survive. My father refused to fight. He was thinking, I am quite sure, of his beloved daughter, and he was wanting to join her in heaven. So he died. He was fifty-seven years old.

My mother had now lost a daughter and a husband all in the space of a few weeks. Heaven knows what it must have

Astri (1912–20)

Olivia (1955–62)

Roald Dahl dedicated **three books** to his beloved daughter Olivia. They were *James and the Giant Peach*, *Fantastic Mr Fox* and *The BFG*.

THE DAHL FAMILY
MONUMENT
In Radyr churchyard, near
their home. It reads:

'In Loving Memory of
Harald Dahl
who died at Tymynydd
April 11th 1920 aged 56
years. And of his daughter
Astri
who died February 13th 1920
aged 7 years.'

felt like to be hit with a double catastrophe like this. Here she was, a young Norwegian in a foreign land, suddenly having to face all alone the very gravest problems and responsibilities. She had five children to look after, three of her own and two by her husband's first wife, and to make matters worse, she herself was expecting another baby in two months' time. A less courageous woman would almost certainly have sold the house and packed her bags and headed straight back to Norway with the children. Over there in her own country she had her mother and father willing and waiting to help her, as well as her two unmarried sisters. But she refused to take the easy way out. Her husband had always stated most emphatically that he wished all his children to be educated in English schools. They were the best in the world, he used to say. Better by far than the Norwegian ones. Better even than the Welsh ones, despite

Me and Mama Radyr

the fact that he lived in Wales and had his business there. He maintained that there was some kind of magic about English schooling and that the education it provided had caused the inhabitants of a small island to become a great nation and a great Empire and to produce the world's greatest literature. 'No child of mine,' he kept saying, 'is going to school anywhere else but in England.' My mother was determined to carry out the wishes of her dead husband.

To accomplish this, she would have to move house from Wales to England, but she wasn't ready for that yet. She must stay here in Wales for a while longer, where she knew people who could help and advise her, especially her husband's great friend and partner, Mr Aadnesen. But even if she wasn't leaving Wales quite yet, it was essential that she move to a smaller and more manageable house. She had enough children to look after without having to bother about a farm as well. So as soon as her fifth child (another daughter) was born, she sold the big house and moved to a smaller one a few miles away in Llandaff. It was called Cumberland Lodge and it was nothing more than a pleasant medium-sized suburban villa. So it was in Llandaff two years later, when I was six years old, that I went to my first school.

me, six

The family moved into **Cumberland Lodge** at some time in late 1921 or early 1922. The house was at **134** **Cardiff Road**, not far from their old home in **Fairwater Road**. It is now part of Howell's School, next door.

The school was a kindergarten run by two sisters, Mrs Corfield and Miss Tucker, and it was called Elmtree House. It is astonishing how little one remembers about one's life before the age of seven or eight. I can tell you all sorts of things that

Roald Dahl and his sister Alfhild were among the first pupils at Elmtree House. The school started in 1922 – with just five pupils!

happened to me from eight onwards, but only very few before that. I went for a whole year to Elmtree House but I cannot even remember what my classroom looked like. Nor can I picture the faces of Mrs Corfield or Miss Tucker, although I am sure they were sweet and smiling. I do have a blurred memory of sitting on the stairs and trying over and over again to tie one of my shoelaces, but that is all that comes back to me at this distance of the school itself.

On the other hand, I can remember very clearly the journeys I made to and from the school because they were so tremendously exciting. Great excitement is probably the only thing that really interests a six-year-old boy and it sticks in his mind. In my case, the excitement centred around my new tricycle. I rode to school on it every day with my eldest sister riding on hers. No grown-ups came with us, and I can remember oh so vividly how the two of us used to go racing at enormous tricycle speeds down the middle of the road and then, most glorious of all, when we came to a corner, we would lean to one side and take it on two wheels. All this, you must realize, was in the good old days when the sight of a motor-car on the street was an event, and it was quite safe for tiny children to go tricycling and whooping their way to school in the centre of the highway.

So much, then, for my memories of kindergarten sixty-two years ago. It's not much, but it's all there is left.

A Grand Time

One of my most enduring memories of early childhood was
my friendship with Joss Spivvis.

It all started in the early nineteen-twenties, not
long after my father and my eldest sister had both died
within a few weeks of one another. The remainder of our
large family, consisting of my mother and six children,
had moved to a house in Llandaff, near Cardiff, which was
called Cumberland Lodge.

The gardener that my mother engaged to look after
everything outdoors was a short, broad-shouldered,
middle-aged Welshman with a pale brown moustache whose
name was Jones. But to us children he very soon became
known as Joss Spivvis, or more often simply Joss. And
very rapidly Joss became a friend to us all, to my
brother and me and my four sisters. Everyone loved him,
but I loved him most of all. I adored him. I worshipped
him, and whenever I was not at school, I used to follow
him around and watch him at his work and listen to him
talk.

Endless stories about his young days Joss would tell
me as I followed him round the garden. In the summer
holidays my mother always took us to Norway, but during
the Christmas and Easter hols I was with Joss all the
time. I never ate lunch in the house with the family. I
ate it with Joss in the harness-room. I would perch on a
sack of maize or a bale of straw while Joss sat rather

grandly in an old kitchen chair that had arms on it.

And there we sat in the quiet of the harness-room while Joss talked and I listened. One of his favourite

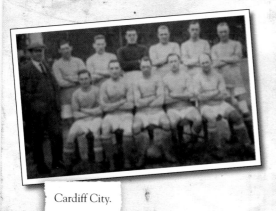

Cardiff City.

subjects was the Cardiff City Football Team, and I was very quickly swept along by his enthusiasm for those heroes of the turf. Cardiff City was a fine club in those days, and if I remember rightly, it was high up in the First Division. Throughout the week, as Saturday came closer and closer, so our excitement grew. The reason was simple. Both of us knew that we were actually going to go to the game together. We always did. Every Saturday afternoon, rain or hail or snow or sleet, Joss and I would go to Ninian Park to see the City play.

Oh, it was a great day, Saturday. Joss would work in the garden until noon, then I would emerge from the house neatly dressed in my scarlet school-cap, my blazer, my flannel shorts and possibly a navy-blue overcoat, and I would hand over to him a half-crown and a shilling that my mother had given me to pay for us both.

'Don't forget to thank your mother,' he would say to me every time as he slipped the two coins into his pocket.

As we rode the twenty-minute journey from Llandaff to Cardiff in the big red bus, our excitement began to mount, and Joss would tell me about the opposing team for that day and the star players in it who were going to threaten our heroes in Cardiff City. It might be Sheffield Wednesday or West Bromwich Albion or Manchester United or any of the fifteen others, and I would listen and remember every detail of what Joss was saying. The bus took us to within five minutes walk of Ninian Park Football Ground, where the great matches were always played, and outside the Ground we would stop at a whelk-stall that stood near the turnstiles. Joss would have a dish of jellied eels (sixpence) and I would have baked beans and two sausages on a cardboard plate (also sixpence).

Then, with an almost unbearable sense of thrill and rapture, and holding Joss tightly by the hand, I would enter the hallowed portals and we would make our way through the crowd to the highest point of the terraces, behind one of the goal-posts. We had to be high up otherwise I wouldn't have seen anything.

But oh, it was thrilling to stand there among those thousands of other men cheering our heroes when they did well and groaning when they lost the ball. We knew all the players by name and to this very day, I can still remember the names of three of them. The

Bill Hardy in flight.

centre-half for Cardiff was a small bald-headed man whom Joss referred to as Little 'Ardy. His name was

Cardiff City played Sheffield United in the FA Cup Final in 1925. Here, Tom Farquarson hurtles across the goal mouth at Wembley.

Hardy. One of the full-backs was Nelson. The goalkeeper was a giant called Farquarson, which my mother told me was pronounced Farkerson, but which Joss pronounced Far-q-arson. Hardy, Nelson and Farquarson. Look up the records and you'll find they were there. And when Cardiff scored a goal, I would jump up and down and Joss would wave his cap in the air, shouting, 'Well played, sir! Well played!'

And after it was all over we would take the bus home again, discussing without pause the great spectacle and the famous men we had just been privileged to see.

It was always dark by the time we reached my house, and Joss, standing in the porch with his cap in his hand, would say to my mother, 'We're back safe, ma'am. We had a grand time.'

Jimmy Nelson being carried off the field after losing the FA Cup Final.

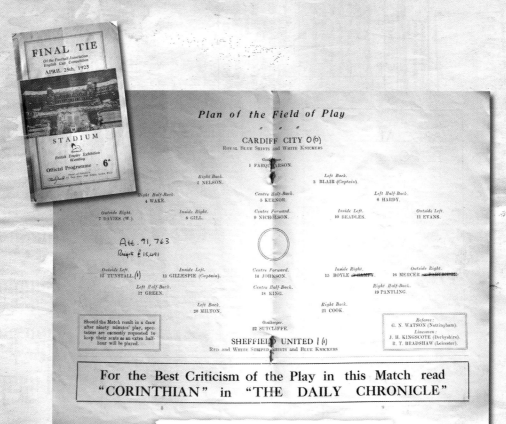

Programme for the FA Cup Final between Cardiff City and Sheffield United in 1925.

Essential facts for (1920s) fans of Cardiff City:

Nickname: The Bluebirds

Strip: Royal blue shirts and white shorts

Ground: Ninian Park, built in 1909

Best year: 1927 – Cardiff won the FA Cup, beating Arsenal 1–0 at Wembley. It was the first football match to be broadcast on radio by the BBC.

..., and is one of the biggest shipbu...
...e capital of Northumbe...

banks of the river being covered on both...
half built ships. ¶

Newcastle has also a very fine coal field) c...

Town rivals Cardiff for the amount of...
countries.

the weather was fine b...

SCOTLAND.

Oslo

Su...

HULL.

Llandaff Cathedral School 1923-5 (age 7-9)

Gosh! FRY'S CHOCOLATE CREAM

ONLY 1D.

Else, me, Alfhild

A picnic with mama

The bicycle and the
sweet-shop

When I was seven, my mother decided I should leave kindergarten and go to a proper boy's school. By good fortune, there existed a well-known Preparatory School for boys about a mile from our house. It was called Llandaff Cathedral School, and it stood right under the shadow of Llandaff cathedral. Like the cathedral, the school is still there and still flourishing.

Although the **Cathedral School** is still going, it moved to new premises in 1958. The buildings which Roald Dahl knew were damaged during an air raid in the **Second World War**.

Llandaff Cathedral

But here again, I can remember very little about the two years I attended Llandaff Cathedral School, between the age

of seven and nine. Only two moments remain clearly in my mind. The first lasted not more than five seconds but I will never forget it.

It was my first term and I was walking home alone across the village green after school when suddenly one of the senior twelve-year-old boys came riding full speed down the road on his bicycle about twenty yards away from me. The road was on a hill and the boy was going down the slope, and as he flashed by he started backpedalling very quickly so that the free-wheeling mechanism of his bike made a loud whirring sound. At the same time, he took his hands off the handlebars and folded them casually across his chest. I stopped dead and stared after him. How wonderful he was! How swift and brave and graceful in his long trousers with bicycle-clips around them and his scarlet school cap at a jaunty angle on his head! One day, I told myself, one glorious day I will have a bike like that and I will wear long trousers with bicycle-clips and my school cap will sit jaunty on my head and I will go whizzing down the hill pedalling backwards with no hands on the handlebars!

I promise you that if somebody had caught me by the shoulder at that moment and said to me, 'What is your greatest wish in life, little boy? What is your absolute ambition? To be a doctor? A fine musician? A painter? A writer? Or the Lord Chancellor?' I would have answered without hesitation that my only ambition, my hope, my longing was to have a bike like that and to go whizzing down the hill with no hands on the handlebars. It would be fabulous. It made me tremble just to think about it.

My second and only other memory of Llandaff Cathedral School is extremely bizarre. It happened a little over a year later, when I was just nine. By then I had made some friends and when I walked to school in the mornings I would start out alone but would pick up four other boys of my own age along the way. After school was over, the same four boys and I would set out together across the village green and through the village itself, heading for home. On the way to school and on the way back we always passed the sweet-shop. No we didn't, we never passed it. We always stopped. We lingered outside its rather small window gazing in at the big glass jars full of Bull's-eyes and Old Fashioned Humbugs and Strawberry Bonbons and Glacier Mints and Acid Drops and Pear Drops and Lemon Drops and all the rest of them. Each of us received sixpence a week for pocket-money, and whenever there was any money in our pockets, we would all troop in together to buy a pennyworth of this or that. My own favourites were Sherbet Suckers and Liquorice Bootlaces.

One of the other boys, whose name was Thwaites, told me I should never eat Liquorice Bootlaces. Thwaites's father, who was a doctor, had said that they were made from rats' blood. The father had given his young son a lecture about Liquorice Bootlaces when he had caught him eating one in bed. 'Every ratcatcher in the country,' the father had said, 'takes his rats to the Liquorice Bootlace Factory, and the manager pays tuppence for each rat. Many a ratcatcher has become a millionaire by selling his dead rats to the Factory.'

'But how do they turn the rats into liquorice?' the young Thwaites had asked his father.

'They wait until they've got ten thousand rats,' the father had answered, 'then they dump them all into a huge shiny steel cauldron and boil them up for several hours. Two men stir the bubbling cauldron with long poles and in the end they have a thick steaming rat-stew. After that, a cruncher is lowered into the cauldron to crunch the bones, and what's left is a pulpy substance called rat-mash.'

liquorice

Bootlaces

'Yes, but how do they turn that into Liquorice Bootlaces, Daddy?' the young Thwaites had asked, and this question, according to Thwaites, had caused his father to pause and think for a few moments before he answered it. At last he had said, 'The two men who were doing the stirring with the long poles now put on their wellington boots and climb into the cauldron and shovel the hot rat-mash out on to a concrete floor. Then they run a steam-roller over it several times to flatten it out. What is left looks rather like a gigantic black pancake, and all they have to do after that is to wait for it to cool and to harden so they can cut it up into strips to make the Bootlaces. Don't ever eat them,' the father had said. 'If you do, you'll get ratitis.'

Ratitis sounds as deadly as Formula 86 Delayed Action Mouse-Maker, a truly nasty spell that appeared in *The Witches*. It is used to turn a child into . . . a mouse!

The bicycle and the sweet-shop

'What is ratitis, Daddy?' young Thwaites had asked.

'All the rats that the rat-catchers catch are poisoned with rat-poison,' the father had said. 'It's the rat-poison that gives you ratitis.'

'Yes, but what happens to you when you catch it?' young Thwaites had asked.

'Your teeth become very sharp and pointed,' the father had answered. 'And a short stumpy tail grows out of your back just above your bottom. There is no cure for ratitis. I ought to know. I'm a doctor.'

We all enjoyed Thwaites's story and we made him tell it to us many times on our walks to and from school. But it didn't stop any of us except Thwaites from buying Liquorice Bootlaces. At two for a penny they were the best value in the shop. A Bootlace, in case you haven't had the pleasure of handling one, is not round. It's like a flat black tape about half an inch wide. You buy it rolled up in a coil, and in those days it used to be so long that when you unrolled it and held one end at arm's length above your head, the other end touched the ground.

Sherbet Suckers were also two a penny. Each Sucker consisted of a yellow cardboard tube filled with sherbet powder, and there was a hollow liquorice straw sticking out of it. (Rat's blood again, young Thwaites would warn us, pointing at the liquorice straw.) You sucked the sherbet up through the straw and when it was finished you ate the liquorice. They were delicious, those Sherbet Suckers. The sherbet fizzed in your mouth, and if you knew how to do it, you could make white froth come out of your nostrils and pretend you were throwing a fit.

Gobstoppers, costing a penny each, were enormous hard round balls the size of small tomatoes. One Gobstopper would

'Bruno was getting smaller by the second. I could see him shrinking . . . Now his clothes seemed to be disappearing and brown fur was growing all over his body . . . Suddenly he had a tail . . . And then he had whiskers . . . Now he had four feet . . . It was all happening so quickly . . . It was a matter of seconds only . . . And all at once he wasn't there any more . . . A small brown mouse was running around on the table top . . .'

An old-fashioned penny would be worth less than half of one pence in today's money.

Roald Dahl simply adored sweets. He **sucked** them, **chewed** them and **crunched** them. And he **wrote** about them whenever he got the chance . . .

'I have always longed and longed to own a sweet-shop. The sweet-shop of my dreams would be loaded from top to bottom with Sherbert Suckers *and* Caramel Fudge *and* Russian Toffee *and* Sugar Snorters *and* Butter Gumballs *and thousands and thousands of other glorious things like that.'*
(The Giraffe and the Pelly and Me)

provide about an hour's worth of non-stop sucking and if you took it out of your mouth and inspected it every five minutes or so, you would find it had changed colour. There was something fascinating about the way it went from pink to blue to green to yellow. We used to wonder how in the world the Gobstopper Factory managed to achieve this magic. 'How *does* it happen?' we would ask each other. 'How *can* they make it keep changing colour?'

'It's your spit that does it,' young Thwaites proclaimed. As the son of a doctor, he considered himself to be an authority on all things that had to do with the body. He could tell us about scabs and when they were ready to be picked off. He knew why a black eye was blue and why blood was red. 'It's your spit that makes a Gobstopper change colour,' he kept insisting. When we asked him to elaborate on this theory, he answered, 'You wouldn't understand it if I did tell you.'

Pear Drops were exciting because they had a dangerous taste. They smelled of nail-varnish and they froze the back of your throat. All of us were warned against eating them, and the result was that we ate them more than ever.

Then there was a hard brown lozenge called the Tonsil Tickler. The Tonsil Tickler tasted and smelled very strongly of chloroform. We had not the slightest doubt that these things were saturated in the dreaded anaesthetic which, as Thwaites had many times pointed out to us, could put you to sleep for hours at a stretch. 'If my father has to saw off somebody's leg,' he said, 'he pours chloroform on to a pad and the person sniffs it and goes to sleep and my father saws his leg off without him even feeling it.'

'But why do they put it into sweets and sell them to us?' we asked him.

You might think a question like this would have baffled Thwaites. But Thwaites was never baffled. 'My father says Tonsil Ticklers were invented for dangerous prisoners in jail,' he said. 'They give them one with each meal and the chloroform makes them sleepy and stops them rioting.'

'Yes,' we said, 'but why sell them to children?'

'It's a plot,' Thwaites said. 'A grown-up plot to keep us quiet.'

The sweet-shop in Llandaff in the year 1923 was the very centre of our lives. To us, it was what a bar is to a drunk, or a church is to a Bishop. Without it, there would have been little to live for. But it had one terrible drawback, this sweet-shop. The woman who owned it was a horror. We hated her and we had good reason for doing so.

Her name was Mrs Pratchett. She was a small skinny old hag with a moustache on her upper lip and a mouth as sour as a green gooseberry. She never smiled. She never welcomed us when we went in, and the only times she spoke were when she said things like, 'I'm watchin' you so keep yer thievin' fingers off them chocolates!' Or 'I don't want you in 'ere just to look around! Either you *forks* out or you *gets* out!'

But by far the most loathsome thing about Mrs Pratchett was the filth that clung around her. Her apron was grey and greasy. Her blouse had bits of breakfast all over it, toast-crumbs and tea stains and splotches of dried egg-yolk. It was her hands, however, that disturbed us most. They were disgusting. They were black with dirt and grime. They looked as though they had been putting lumps of coal on the fire all day long. And do not

There were at least **three sweet-shops** in Llandaff when Roald Dahl was a boy. He passed two of these gloriously **sweet** and **sticky emporiums** on his way to and from school. That's four sweet-shops a day, five days a week. It's no wonder he couldn't resist.

Two of Roald Dahl's most foul characters were the Twits, Mrs Twit especially. Perhaps she was inspired by a certain Mrs Pratchett?

'. . . Mrs Twit wasn't born ugly. She'd had quite a nice face when she was young. The ugliness had grown upon her year by year as she got older.

Why would that happen? I'll tell you why.

If a person has ugly thoughts, it begins to show on the face. And when that person has ugly thoughts every day, every week, every year, the face gets uglier and uglier until it gets so ugly you can hardly bear to look at it.'
(The Twits)

forget please that it was these very hands and fingers that she plunged into the sweet-jars when we asked for a pennyworth of Treacle Toffee or Wine Gums or Nut Clusters or whatever. There were precious few health laws in those days, and nobody, least of all Mrs Pratchett, ever thought of using a little shovel for getting out the sweets as they do today. The mere sight of her grimy right hand with its black fingernails digging an ounce of Chocolate Fudge out of a jar would have caused a starving tramp to go running from the shop. But not us. Sweets were our life-blood. We would have put up with far worse than that to get them. So we simply stood and watched in sullen silence while this disgusting old woman stirred around inside the jars with her foul fingers.

The other thing we hated Mrs Pratchett for was her meanness. Unless you spent a whole sixpence all in one go, she wouldn't give you a bag. Instead you got your sweets twisted up in a small piece of newspaper which she tore off a pile of old *Daily Mirrors* lying on the counter.

So you can well understand that we had it in for Mrs Pratchett in a big way, but we didn't quite know what to do about it. Many schemes were put forward but none of them was any good. None of them, that is, until suddenly, one memorable afternoon, we found the dead mouse.

The Great Mouse Plot

My four friends and I had come across a loose floor-board at the back of the classroom, and when we prised it up with the blade of a pocket-knife, we discovered a big hollow space underneath. This, we decided, would be our secret hiding place for sweets and other small treasures such as conkers and monkey-nuts and birds' eggs. Every afternoon, when the last lesson was over, the five of us would wait until the classroom had emptied, then we would lift up the floor-board and examine our secret hoard, perhaps adding to it or taking something away.

One day, when we lifted it up, we found a dead mouse lying among our treasures. It was an exciting discovery. Thwaites took it out by its tail and waved it in front of our faces. 'What shall we do with it?' he cried.

'It stinks!' someone shouted. 'Throw it out of the window quick!'

'Hold on a tick,' I said. 'Don't throw it away.'

Thwaites hesitated. They all looked at me.

When writing about oneself, one must strive to be truthful. Truth is more imporant than modesty. I must tell you, therefore, that it was I and I alone who had the idea for the great and daring Mouse Plot. We all have our moments of brilliance and glory, and this was mine.

'Why don't we,' I said, 'slip it into one of Mrs Pratchett's jars of sweets? Then when she puts her dirty hand in to grab a handful, she'll grab a stinky dead mouse instead.'

The other four stared at me in wonder. Then, as the sheer genius of the plot began to sink in, they all started grinning. They slapped me on the back. They cheered me and danced around the classroom. 'We'll do it today!' they cried. 'We'll do it on the way home! *You* had the idea,' they said to me, 'so *you* can be the one to put the mouse in the jar.'

Thwaites handed me the mouse. I put it into my trouser pocket. Then the five of us left the school, crossed the village green and headed for the sweet-shop. We were tremendously jazzed up. We felt like a gang of desperados setting out to rob a train or blow up the sheriff's office.

'Make sure you put it into a jar which is used often,' somebody said.

'I'm putting it in Gobstoppers,' I said. 'The Gobstopper jar is never behind the counter.'

'I've got a penny,' Thwaites said, 'so I'll ask for one Sherbet Sucker and one Bootlace. And while she turns away to get them, you slip the mouse in quickly with the Gobstoppers.'

Thus everything was arranged. We were strutting a little as we entered the shop. We were the victors now and Mrs Pratchett was the victim. She stood behind the counter, and her small malignant pig-eyes watched us suspiciously as we came forward.

'One Sherbet Sucker, please,' Thwaites said to her, holding out his penny.

I kept to the rear of the group, and when I saw Mrs Pratchett turn her head away for a couple of seconds to fish a

Sherbet Sucker out of the box, I lifted the heavy glass lid of the Gobstopper jar and dropped the mouse in. Then I replaced the lid as silently as possible. My heart was thumping like mad and my hands had gone all sweaty.

'And one Bootlace, please,' I heard Thwaites saying. When I turned round, I saw Mrs Pratchett holding out the Bootlace in her filthy fingers.

'I don't want all the lot of you troopin' in 'ere if only one of you is buyin',' she screamed at us. 'Now beat it! Go on, get out!'

As soon as we were outside, we broke into a run. 'Did you do it?' they shouted at me.

'Of course I did!' I said.

'Well done you!' they cried. 'What a super show!'

I felt like a hero. I *was* a hero. It was marvellous to be so popular.

The flush of triumph over the dead mouse was carried forward to the next morning as we all met again to walk to school.

'Let's go in and see if it's still in the jar,' somebody said as we approached the sweet-shop.

'Don't,' Thwaites said firmly. 'It's too dangerous. Walk past as though nothing has happened.'

As we came level with the shop we saw a cardboard notice hanging on the door.

We stopped and stared. We had never known the sweet-shop to be closed at this time in the morning, even on Sundays.

'What's happened?' we asked each other. 'What's going on?'

We pressed our faces against the window and looked inside. Mrs Pratchett was nowhere to be seen.

'Look!' I cried. 'The Gobstopper jar's gone! It's not on the shelf! There's a gap where it used to be!'

'It's on the floor!' someone said. 'It's smashed to bits and there's Gobstoppers everywhere!'

'There's the mouse!' someone else shouted.

We could see it all, the huge glass jar smashed to smithereens with the dead mouse lying in the wreckage and hundreds of many-coloured Gobstoppers littering the floor.

'She got such a shock when she grabbed hold of the mouse that she dropped everything,' somebody was saying.

'But why didn't she sweep it all up and open the shop?' I asked.

Nobody answered me.

We turned away and walked towards the school. All of a sudden we had begun to feel slightly uncomfortable. There was something not quite right about the shop being closed. Even Thwaites was unable to offer a reasonable explanation. We became silent. There was a faint scent of danger in the air now. Each one of us had caught a whiff of it. Alarm bells were beginning to ring faintly in our ears.

After a while, Thwaites broke the silence. 'She must have got one heck of a shock,' he said. He paused. We all looked at him, wondering what wisdom the great medical authority was going to come out with next.

'After all,' he went on, 'to catch hold of a dead mouse when you're expecting to catch hold of a Gobstopper must be a pretty frightening experience. Don't you agree?'

Nobody answered him.

'Well now,' Thwaites went on, 'when an old person like Mrs Pratchett suddenly gets a very big shock, I suppose you know what happens next?'

'What?' we said. 'What happens?'

'You ask my father,' Thwaites said. 'He'll tell you.'

'You tell us,' we said.

'It gives her a heart attack,' Thwaites announced. 'Her heart stops beating and she's dead in five seconds.'

For a moment or two my own heart stopped beating. Thwaites pointed a finger at me and said darkly, 'I'm afraid you've killed her.'

'*Me?*' I cried. 'Why just *me?*'

'It was *your* idea,' he said. 'And what's more, *you* put the mouse in.'

All of a sudden, I was a murderer.

At exactly that point, we heard the school bell ringing in the distance and we had to gallop the rest of the way so as not to be late for prayers.

Prayers were held in the Assembly Hall. We all perched in rows on wooden benches while the teachers sat up on the platform in armchairs, facing us. The five of us scrambled into our places just as the Headmaster marched in, followed by the rest of the staff.

The Headmaster is the only teacher at Llandaff Cathedral School that I can remember, and for a reason you will soon discover, I can remember him very clearly indeed. His name was Mr Coombes and I have a picture in my mind of a giant of a man with a face like a ham and a mass of rusty-coloured hair that sprouted in a tangle all over the top of his head. All grown-ups appear as giants to small children. But

Headmasters (and policemen) are the biggest giants of all and acquire a marvellously exaggerated stature. It is possible that Mr Coombes was a perfectly normal being, but in my memory he was a giant, a tweed-suited giant who always wore a black gown over his tweeds and a waistcoat under his jacket.

Mr Coombes now proceeded to mumble through the same old prayers we had every day, but this morning, when the last amen had been spoken, he did not turn and lead his group rapidly out of the Hall as usual. He remained standing before us, and it was clear he had an announcement to make.

'The whole school is to go out and line up around the playground immediately,' he said. 'Leave your books behind. And no talking.'

Mr Coombes was looking grim. His hammy pink face had taken on that dangerous scowl which only appeared when he was extremely cross and somebody was for the high-jump. I sat there small and frightened among the rows and rows of other boys, and to me at that moment the Headmaster, with his black gown draped over his shoulders, was like a judge at a murder trial.

'He's after the killer,' Thwaites whispered to me.

I began to shiver.

'I'll bet the police are here already,' Thwaites went on. 'And the Black Maria's waiting outside.'

As we made our way out to the playground, my whole stomach began to feel as though it was slowly filling up with swirling water. *I am only eight years old*, I told myself. *No little boy of eight has ever murdered anyone. It's not possible.*

Out in the playground on this warm cloudy September morning, the Deputy Headmaster was shouting, 'Line up in forms! Sixth Form over there! Fifth Form next to them! Spread out! Spread out! Get on with it! Stop talking all of you!'

Thwaites and I and my other three friends were in the Second Form, the lowest but one, and we lined up against the red-brick wall of the playground shoulder to shoulder. I can remember that when every boy in the school was in his place, the line stretched right round the four sides of the playground – about one hundred small boys altogether, aged between six and twelve, all of us wearing identical grey shorts and grey blazers and grey stockings and black shoes.

'Stop that *talking*!' shouted the Deputy Head. 'I want absolute silence!'

But why for heaven't sake were we in the playground at all? I wondered. And why were we lined up like this? It had never happened before.

I half-expected to see two policemen come bounding out of the school to grab me by the arms and put handcuffs on my wrists.

A single door led out from the school on to the playground. Suddenly it swung open and through it, like the angel of death, strode Mr Coombes, huge and bulky in his tweed suit and black gown, and beside him, believe it or not, right beside him trotted the tiny figure of Mrs Pratchett herself!

Mrs Pratchett was alive!

The relief was tremendous.

'She's alive!' I whispered to Thwaites standing next to me. 'I didn't kill her!' Thwaites ignored me.

'We'll start over here,' Mr Coombes was saying to Mrs Pratchett. He grasped her by one of her skinny arms and led her over to where the Sixth Form was standing. Then, still keeping hold of her arm, he proceeded to lead her at a brisk walk down the line of boys. It was like someone inspecting the troops.

'What on earth are they doing?' I whispered.

Thwaites didn't answer me. I glanced at him. He had gone rather pale.

'Too big,' I heard Mrs Pratchett saying. 'Much too big. It's none of this lot. Let's 'ave a look at some of them titchy ones.'

Mr Coombes increased his pace. 'We'd better go all the way round,' he said. He seemed in a hurry to get it over with now and I could see Mrs Pratchett's skinny goat's legs trotting to keep up with him. They had already inspected one side of the playground where the Sixth Form and half the Fifth Form were standing. We watched them moving down the second side . . . then the third side.

'Still too big,' I heard Mrs Pratchett croaking. 'Much too big! Smaller than these! Much smaller! Where's them nasty little ones?'

They were coming closer to us now . . . closer and closer.

They were starting on the fourth side . . .

Every boy in our form was watching Mr Coombes and Mrs Pratchett as they came walking down the line towards us.

'Nasty cheeky lot, these little 'uns!' I heard Mrs Pratchett muttering. 'They comes into my shop and they thinks they can do what they damn well likes!'

Mr Coombes made no reply to this.

'They nick things when I ain't lookin',' she went on. 'They put their grubby 'ands all over everything and they've got no manners. I don't mind girls. I never 'ave no trouble with girls, but boys is 'ideous and 'orrible! I don't 'ave to tell *you* that, 'Eadmaster, do I?'

'These are the smaller ones,' Mr Coombes said.

I could see Mrs Pratchett's piggy little eyes staring hard at the face of each boy she passed.

Suddenly she let out a high-pitched yell and pointed a dirty finger straight at Thwaites. 'That's 'im!' she yelled. 'That's one of 'em! I'd know 'im a mile away, the scummy little bounder!'

The entire school turned to look at Thwaites. 'W-what have *I* done?' he stuttered, appealing to Mr Coombes.

'Shut up,' Mr Coombes said.

Mrs Pratchett's eyes flicked over and settled on my own face. I looked down and studied the black asphalt surface of the playground.

''Ere's another of 'em!' I heard her yelling. 'That one there!' She was pointing at me now.

'You're quite sure?' Mr Coombes said.

'Of course I'm sure!' she cried. 'I never forgets a face, least of all when it's as sly as that! 'Ee's one of 'em all right! There was five altogether! Now where's them other three?'

The other three, as I knew very well, were coming up next.

Mrs Pratchett's face was glimmering with venom as her eyes travelled beyond me down the line.

'There they are!' she cried out, stabbing the air with her finger. ''Im . . . and 'im . . . and 'im! That's the five of 'em all right! We don't need to look no farther than this, 'Eadmaster! They're all 'ere, the nasty dirty little pigs! You've got their names, 'ave you?'

'I've got their names, Mrs Pratchett,' Mr Coombes told her. 'I'm much obliged to you.'

'And I'm much obliged to *you*, 'Eadmaster,' she answered.

As Mr Coombes led her away across the playground, we heard her saying, 'Right in the jar of Gobstoppers it was! A stinkin' dead mouse which I will never forget as long as I live!'

'You have my deepest sympathy,' Mr Coombes was muttering.

'Talk about shocks!' she went on. 'When my fingers caught

'old of that nasty soggy stinkin' dead mouse . . .' Her voice trailed away as Mr Coombes led her quickly through the door into the school building.

Our form master came into the classroom with a piece of paper in his hand. 'The following are to report to the Headmaster's study at once,' he said. 'Thwaites . . . Dahl . . .' And then he read out the other three names which I have forgotten.

The five of us stood up and left the room. We didn't speak as we made our way down the long corridor into the Headmaster's private quarters where the dreaded study was situated. Thwaites knocked on the door.

'Enter!'

We sidled in. The room smelled of leather and tobacco. Mr Coombes was standing in the middle of it, dominating everything, a giant of a man if ever there was one, and in his hands he held a long yellow cane which curved round the top like a walking stick.

the cane

'I don't want any lies,' he said. 'I know very well you did it and you were all in it together. Line up over there against the bookcase.'

We lined up, Thwaites in front and I, for some reason, at the very back. I was last in the line.

'You,' Mr Coombes said, pointing the cane at Thwaites, 'Come over here.'

Thwaites went forward very slowly.

'Bend over,' Mr Coombes said.

Thwaites bent over. Our eyes were riveted on him. We were hypnotized by it all. We knew, of course, that boys got the cane now and again, but we had never heard of anyone being made to watch.

'Tighter, boy, tighter!' Mr Coombes snapped out. 'Touch the ground!'

Thwaites touched the carpet with the tips of his fingers.

Mr Coombes stood back and took up a firm stance with his legs well apart. I thought how small Thwaites's bottom looked and how very tight it was. Mr Coombes had his eyes focused squarely upon it. He raised the cane high above his shoulder, and as he brought it down, it made a loud swishing sound, and then there was a crack like a pistol shot as it struck Thwaites's bottom.

Little Thwaites seemed to lift about a foot into the air and he yelled 'Ow-w-w-w-w-w-w-w-w!' and straightened up like elastic.

'"Arder!' shrieked a voice from over in the corner.

Now it was our turn to jump. We looked round and there, sitting in one of Mr Coombes's big leather armchairs, was the tiny loathsome figure of Mrs Pratchett! She was bounding up and down with excitement. 'Lay it into 'im!' she was shrieking. 'Let 'im 'ave it! Teach 'im a lesson!'

'Get down, boy!' Mr Coombes ordered. 'And stay down! You get an extra one every time you straighten up!'

'That's tellin' 'im!' shrieked Mrs Pratchett. 'That's tellin' the little blighter!'

I could hardly believe what I was seeing. It was like some awful pantomime. The violence was bad enough, and being made to watch it was even worse, but with Mrs Pratchett in the audience the whole thing became a nightmare.

Swish-crack! went the cane.

'Ow-w-w-w-w!' yelled Thwaites.

'"Arder!' shrieked Mrs Pratchett. 'Stitch 'im up! Make it

sting! Tickle 'im up good and proper! Warm 'is backside for 'im! Go on, warm it up, 'Eadmaster!'

Thwaites received four strokes, and by gum, they were four real whoppers.

'Next!' snapped Mr Coombes.

Thwaites came hopping past us on his toes, clutching his bottom with both hands and yelling, 'Ow! Ouch! Ouch! Ouch! Owwwww!'

With tremendous reluctance, the next boy sidled forward to his fate. I stood there wishing I hadn't been last in the line. The watching and waiting were probably even greater torture than the event itself.

Mr Coombes's performance the second time was the same as the first. So was Mrs Pratchett's. She kept up her screeching all the way through, exhorting Mr Coombes to greater and still greater efforts, and the awful thing was that he seemed to be responding to her cries. He was like an athlete who is spurred on by the shouts of the crowd in the stands. Whether this was true or not, I was sure of one thing. He wasn't weakening.

My own turn came at last. My mind was swimming and my eyes had gone all blurry as I went forward to bend over. I can remember wishing my mother would suddenly come bursting into the room shouting, 'Stop! How dare you do that to my son!' But she didn't. All I heard was Mrs Pratchett's dreadful high-pitched voice behind me screeching, 'This one's the cheekiest of the bloomin' lot, 'Eadmaster! Make sure you let 'im 'ave it good and strong!'

Mr Coombes did just that. As the first stroke landed and the pistol-crack sounded, I was thrown forward so violently that if my fingers hadn't been touching the carpet, I think I would have fallen flat on my face. As it was, I was able to catch myself on the palms of my hands and keep my balance. At first I heard only the *crack* and felt absolutely nothing at all, but a fraction of a second later the burning sting that flooded across my buttocks was so terrific that all I could do was gasp. I gave a great gushing gasp that emptied my lungs of every breath of air that was in them.

It felt, I promise you, as though someone had laid a red-hot poker against my flesh and was pressing down on it hard.

The second stroke was worse than the first and this was probably because Mr Coombes was well practised and had a splendid aim. He was able, so it seemed, to land the second one almost exactly across the narrow line where the first one had struck. It is bad enough when the cane lands on fresh skin, but when it comes down on bruised and wounded flesh, the agony is unbelievable.

The third one seemed even worse than the second. Whether or not the wily Mr Coombes had chalked the cane beforehand and had thus made an aiming mark on my grey flannel shorts after the first stroke, I do not know. I am inclined to doubt it because he must have known that this was a practice much frowned upon by Headmasters in general in those days. It was not only regarded as unsporting, it was also an admission that you were not an expert at the job.

By the time the fourth stroke was delivered, my entire backside seemed to be going up in flames.

Far away in the distance, I heard Mr Coombes's voice saying, 'Now get out.'

As I limped across the study clutching my buttocks hard with both hands, a cackling sound came from the armchair over in the corner, and then I heard the vinegary voice of Mrs Pratchett saying, 'I am much obliged to you, 'Eadmaster, very much obliged. I don't think we is goin' to see any more stinkin' mice in my Gobstoppers from now on.'

When I returned to the classroom my eyes were wet with tears and everybody stared at me. My bottom hurt when I sat down at my desk.

That evening after supper my three sisters had their baths before me. Then it was my turn, but as I was about to step into the bathtub, I heard a horrified gasp from my mother behind me.

'What's this?' she gasped. 'What's happened to you?' She was staring at my bottom. I myself had not inspected it up to then, but when I twisted my head around and took a look at one of my buttocks, I saw the scarlet stripes and the deep blue bruising in between.

'Who did this?' my mother cried. 'Tell me at once!'

In the end I had to tell her the whole story, while my three sisters (aged nine, six and four) stood around in their nighties listening goggle-eyed. My mother heard me out in silence. She asked no questions. She just let me talk, and when I had finished, she said to our nurse, 'You get them into bed, Nanny. I'm going out.'

If I had had the slightest idea of what she was going to do next, I would have tried to stop her, but I hadn't. She went straight downstairs and put on her hat. Then she marched out of the house, down the drive and on to the road. I saw her through my bedroom window as she went out of the gates and turned left, and I remember calling out to her to come back, come back, come back. But she took no notice of me. She was walking very quickly, with her head held high and her body erect, and by the look of things I figured that Mr Coombes was in for a hard time.

About an hour later, my mother returned and came upstairs to kiss us all goodnight. 'I wish you hadn't done that,' I said to her. 'It makes me look silly.'

'They don't beat small children like that where I come from,' she said. 'I won't allow it.'

'What did Mr Coombes say to you, Mama?'

'He told me I was a foreigner and I didn't understand how British schools were run,' she said.

'Did he get ratty with you?'

'Very ratty,' she said. 'He told me that if I didn't like his methods I could take you away.'

'What did you say?'

'I said I would, as soon as the school year is finished. I shall find you an *English* school this time,' she said. 'Your father was right. English schools are the best in the world.'

'Does that mean it'll be a boarding school?' I asked.

'It'll have to be,' she said. 'I'm not quite ready to move the whole family to England yet.'

So I stayed on at Llandaff Cathedral School until the end of the summer term.

A Life Without Sweets

Life without the sweet-shop and without sweets would hardly be worth living. It wouldn't be worth living. Gone for ever would be the thrill of jingling the pennies in one's pockets all through the day and wondering exactly how to spend them. I myself had often whiled away an entire arithmetic lesson wondering just how to get the best possible value out of a single penny in the sweet-shop on the way home. Would it be two Liquorice Bootlaces? Or would it be one Bootlace and one Sherbert Sucker? Or should I blow it all on a Gobstopper? The advantage of the Gobstopper was that you could make it last almost for ever by sucking it for only a few minutes at a time and then taking it out and putting it in your handkerchief. Perhaps, yes perhaps it might be better to spend it on Aniseed Balls, which were six for a penny. Would six Aniseed Balls last longer than one Gobstopper? Grappling with questions such as these could furrow my brow for hour after hour.

'We simply can't go without sweets for the rest of our lives!' I cried.

We stood there gazing across the street at the sweet-shop.

Thwaites was tinkling some pennies in his pocket. I had two halfpennies in mine and was running my fingers lovingly around them. It was simply terrible standing there like that. It was hell on earth. It was pure torture.

But the thing about torture is that it concentrates the mind most marvellously. I could feel my own mind beginning to concentrate at this very moment. Massive brainwaves were starting to surge through my head.

'I think I may have a bit of an idea,' I said softly.

'No, thank you!' they cried. 'Don't tell us! We don't want any more of your rotten ideas! You had a beauty yesterday, didn't you, and look where it landed us!'

'This one is safe,' I said.

'Keep it to yourself,' they told me.

'It's a wheeze for getting our own back on Mrs Pratchett,' I said, 'and for getting something to eat at the same time.'

'How can we possibly get our own back on Mrs Pratchett?' somebody said.

'I suppose you want us to throw a brick through her window?' someone else said.

'I told you this one is safe,' I said. 'We won't be breaking a single rule. And we'll get some eats into the bargain.'

I saw them hesitate.

I proceeded to tell them about my great and brilliant Chocolate-Mouse Plan.

'By golly,' Thwaites said grudgingly when I had finished. 'I must say, it would be a bit of a lark.'

* * *

As we walked slowly across the road towards
the sweet-shop, that famous old tingle of
excitement came flooding over me once again.
I loved that feeling. I craved it. It was an
addiction. I got it, for example, when I went
birds-nesting up a very tall tree that had
long branches. I got it when swinging
on a swing standing up and going so
high that the ropes went slack at the
top of the swing. I got it when eating
in class because if they caught you you
were always sent straight to the Headmaster
who caned you on the spot. I got it on
the second-floor balcony of our house when
tightrope walking along the top rail with a
fall of twenty feet on one side. I got it
from doing lots of other things and I was
getting it now as we walked across the
road towards Mrs Pratchett's sweet-
shop. The tension was terrible. I
hoped it would last.
  'Ha!' Mrs Pratchett said as the five
of us sidled in. 'So you've come to
say you're sorry, 'ave you? And so you ruddy
well should be!' She rubbed her filthy hands
together and started to cackle. 'I'll bet
them little backsides of yours is smartin'
something fierce!' she went on. ''E does a
very neat job, that 'eadmaster of yours, when
'e puts 'is mind to it, ain't that so?'
  We kept silent. We lined up in an orderly
queue in front of the counter, and we placed
ourselves in the same order we had been in,

in Mr Coombes's study, with Thwaites first and me last. No one of us grinned or giggled. We kept our faces absolutely solemn and we did our best to look like angels.

'We, we are a nice well-be'aved little bunch this afternoon, ain't we?' she went on. 'There's nothin' like a few good ticklers on the rump to take the cheekiness out of you. It works bloomin' miracles, don't it just!'

She was gloating over us and thoroughly enjoying herself. Not one of us made a murmur. We simply stood there quietly and waited for her to have her say.

'I knows one thing,' she announced. 'We won't be 'avin' no more talk about mice after what's 'appened today and that's for sure!'

This was Thwaites' cue. 'One mouse, please,' he said politely, holding out his halfpenny.

This pulled her up short. She looked very carefully into his face, searching for the smirk. 'One what?' she screeched.

'One mouse, please,' Thwaites repeated. 'One chocolate mouse.'

'You cheeky little blighter!' she cried. 'You're tryin' to 'ave me on, ain't you?'

'Here's the money,' Thwaites said. 'I'd like a mouse.'

Mrs Pratchett stood there glaring at little Thwaites. She was completely off balance now. She knew that he had every right to ask for a chocolate mouse if he wanted one. Very slowly she took the halfpenny and slid the chocolate mouse across the glass counter with her dirty fingers. 'And what do you want?' she said to the next boy in line.

'I want a mouse, too,' he said.

Mrs Pratchett's face went the colour of a ripe plum. 'You've got a flamin' nerve!' she cried. 'I'll report you for this!'

'What for?' the boy asked. 'I've not done anything wrong. I want to buy a chocolate mouse. They are for sale, aren't they?'

'I suppose you're all wantin' mice?' she screeched at us. 'So that's the game, is it?'

'Yes, please,' we said, holding out our halfpennies. 'A mouse for me . . . and a mouse for me and . . . a mouse for me.'

'You're tryin' to make a mock of me!' she cried. 'You've never bought no mice before, not one of you! You're tryin' to pull my flamin' leg!'

We kept our nerve. Not a smile nor a smirk touched our lips. 'It's a sort of mousey day for us today,' I said to her. 'So we thought we'd celebrate by having chocolate ones. There's nothing wrong with that, is there?'

She pursed her lips up tight and said nothing. We had her beaten and she knew it. She took four more mice out of the box and threw them on the counter. We put down our money and picked up the mice.

'Thank you,' we said. 'Thank you, thank you. Goodbye, Mrs Pratchett.'

'Beat it!' she screeched. ''Op it! Get out of 'ere, the lot of you!'

It was a famous victory. Outside on the road, we did a little jig of delight, and then we walked back to our separate homes, each munching his chocolate mouse.

If *you* go on holiday to Norway, you'll need to know these *very* important words:

hallo – *hello*

Hvordan har du det?
– *How are you?*

Takk, bare bra.
– *Very well, thank you*

fjord – *inlet*

tivoli – *amusement pa*

OSLO. SEPT. 5TH.
Oslo is the capital of Norway.
It used to be one of the centres of the Vikings who used to raid
the East coast of England so mercilisusly in the days of King Alfred
Its chief export is wood, used for pit-props and matches.
The weather was very warm indeed.
The capital, unlike London
is kept extremely clean, and any
one found dropping a piece of paper
in the streets is summoned, at once.
Thus the streets are kept wonderfully clean.
NORWAY.
Oslo.
SWEDEN.
NORTH
SEA.
Newcastle.
ROUTE.
ENGLAND.
HULL

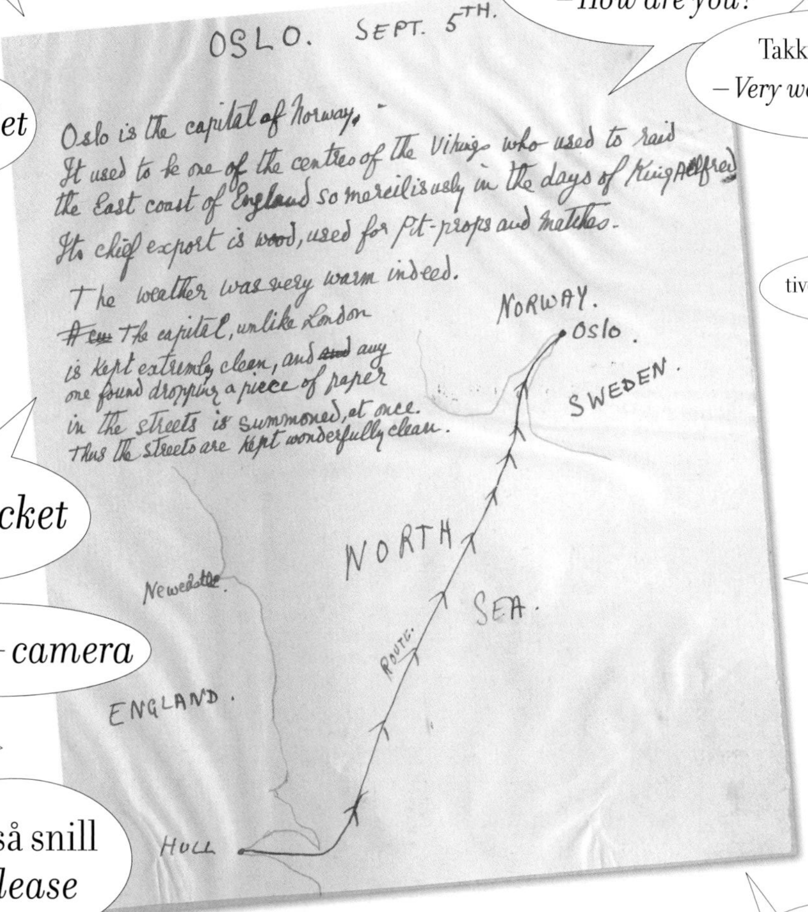

bøtte – *bucket*

Jeg vil gjerne
en kopp t
– *I would li*
cup of te

kamera – *camera*

vær så snill
– *please*

tusen takk
– *thank you*

skaal! – *cheers!*

kringle –
a type of pastry

bare hyggelig
– *my pleasure*

ha det bra – *goodbye*

Going to Norway

The summer holidays! Those magic words! The mere mention of them used to send shivers of joy rippling over my skin.

All my summer holidays, from when I was four years old to when I was seventeen (1920 to 1932), were totally idyllic. This, I am certain, was because we always went to the same idyllic place and that place was Norway.

Except for my ancient half-sister and my not-quite-so-ancient half-brother, the rest of us were all pure Norwegian by blood. We all spoke Norwegian and all our relations lived over there. So in a way, going to Norway every summer was like going home.

Even the journey was an event. Do not forget that there were no commercial aeroplanes in those times, so it took us four whole days to complete the trip out and another four days to get home again.

The Harbour, Rossesund, Norway.

This was the gateway to Roald's summer holidays. The steamer left from here, its destination the beautiful island of Tjöme.

59

Getting off the ferry.

THE PRINCIPLE STREET.
ROYAL PALACE IN BACKGROUND.

THE ROYAL PALACE.

Roald Dahl made this scrapbook when he was about thirteen. It details all the journeys made by the family during one summer holiday to Norway.

We were always an enormous party. There were my three sisters and my ancient half-sister (that's four), and my half-brother and me (that's six), and my mother (that's seven), and Nanny (that's eight), and in addition to these, there were never less than two others who were some sort of anonymous ancient friends of the ancient half-sister (that's ten altogether).

Looking back on it now, I don't know how my mother did it. There were all those train bookings and boat bookings and hotel bookings to be made in advance by letter. She had to make sure that we had enough shorts and shirts and sweaters and gymshoes and bathing costumes (you couldn't even buy a shoelace on the island we were going to), and the packing must have been a nightmare. Six huge trunks were carefully packed, as well as countless suitcases, and when the great departure day arrived, the ten of us, together with our mountains of luggage, would set out on the first and easiest step of the journey, the train to London.

When we arrived in London, we tumbled into three taxis and went clattering across the great city to King's Cross, where we got on to the train for Newcastle, two hundred miles to the north. The trip to Newcastle took about five hours, and when we arrived there, we needed three more taxis to take us from the station to the docks, where our boat would be waiting. The next stop after that would be Oslo, the capital of Norway.

When I was young, the capital of Norway was not called Oslo. It was called Christiania. But somewhere along the line, the Norwegians decided to do away with that pretty name and call it Oslo instead. As children, we always knew it as Christiania, but if I call it that here we shall only get confused, so I had better stick to Oslo all the way through.

The sea journey from Newcastle to Oslo took two days and a night, and if it was rough, as it often was, all of us got seasick except our dauntless mother. We used to lie in deck-chairs on the promenade deck, within easy reach of the rails, embalmed in rugs, our faces slate-grey and our stomachs churning, refusing the hot soup and ship's biscuits the kindly steward kept offering us. And as for poor Nanny, she began to feel sick the moment she set foot on deck. 'I hate these things!' she used to say. 'I'm sure we'll never get there! Which lifeboat do we go to when it starts to sink?' Then she would retire to her cabin, where she stayed groaning and trembling until the ship was firmly tied up at the quayside in Oslo harbour the next day.

We always stopped off for one night in Oslo so that we could have a grand annual family reunion with Bestemama and Bestepapa, our mother's parents, and with her two maiden sisters (our aunts) who lived in the same house.

When we got off the boat, we all went in a cavalcade of taxis straight to the Grand Hotel, where we would sleep one night, to drop off our luggage. Then, keeping the same taxis, we drove on to the grandparents' house, where an emotional welcome awaited us. All of us were embraced and kissed many times and tears flowed down wrinkled old cheeks and suddenly that quiet gloomy house came alive with many children's voices.

Ever since I first saw her, Bestemama was terrifically ancient. She was a white-haired wrinkly-faced old bird who seemed always to be sitting in her rocking-chair, rocking away and smiling benignly at this vast influx of grandchildren who barged in from miles away to take over her house for a few hours every year.

Roald Dahl's Bestemama and Grandmamma from *The Witches* are curiously alike . . .

'My grandmother was tremendously old and wrinkled, with a massive wide body which was smothered in grey lace. She sat there majestic in her armchair, filling every inch of it. Not even a mouse could have squeezed in to sit beside her.'

61

Bestepapa was the quiet one. He was a small dignified scholar with a white goatee beard, and as far as I could gather, he was an astrologer, a meteorologist and a speaker of ancient Greek. Like Bestemama, he sat most of the time quietly in a chair, saying very little and totally overwhelmed, I imagine, by the raucous rabble who were destroying his neat and polished home. The two things I remember most about Bestepapa were that he wore black boots and that he smoked an extraordinary pipe. The bowl of his pipe was made of meerschaum clay, and it had a flexible stem about three feet long so that the bowl rested on his lap.

Bestepapa Hesselberg.

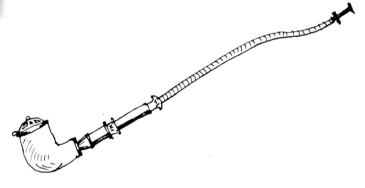

All the grown-ups including Nanny, and all the children, even when the youngest was only a year old, sat down around the big oval dining-room table on the afternoon of our arrival, for the great annual celebration feast with the grandparents, and the food we received never varied. This was a Norwegian household, and for the Norwegians the best food in the world is fish. And when they say fish, they don't mean the sort of thing you and I get from the fishmonger. They mean *fresh fish*, fish that has been caught no more than twenty-four hours before and has never been frozen or chilled on a block of ice. I agree with them that the proper way to prepare fish like this is to poach it, and that is what they do with the finest specimens. And Norwegians, by the way, always eat the skin of the boiled fish, which they say has the best taste of all.

(From left to right)
Bestepapa Hesselberg,
Bestemama Hesselberg,
Tante Ellen, Tante Astri
(Tante = 'aunt') with Roald
Dahl's sister Astri on a
rocking horse.

So naturally this great celebration feast started with fish. A massive fish, a flounder as big as a tea-tray and as thick as your arm was brought to the table. It had nearly black skin on top which was covered with brilliant orange spots, and it had, of course, been perfectly poached. Large white hunks of this fish were carved out and put on to our plates, and with it we had hollandaise sauce and boiled new potatoes. Nothing else. And by gosh, it was delicious.

As soon as the remains of the fish had been cleared away, a tremendous craggy mountain of home-made ice-cream would be carried in. Apart from being the creamiest ice-cream in the world, the flavour was unforgettable. There were thousands of little chips of crisp burnt toffee mixed into it (the Norwegians call it *krokan*), and as a result it didn't simply melt in your mouth like ordinary ice-cream. You chewed it and it went *crunch* and the taste was something you dreamed about for days afterwards.

KROKAN ICE-CREAM

Ingredients
30g butter
60g sweet almonds, roughly chopped
5g bitter almonds, finely chopped
150g sugar
A tub of vanilla ice-cream

1. Smooth a piece of foil over a baking tray and lightly grease it.
2. Place the butter, almonds and sugar in a heavy frying pan.
3. Put pan over a moderate heat, stirring all the time to make sure that the mixture doesn't burn.
4. When the mixture has turned a golden colour, pour it on to the greased foil.
5. Allow to cool completely before peeling off the foil.
6. Put the hardened krokan into a freezer bag and lightly crush into small pieces with a rolling pin.
7. Take the ice-cream out of the fridge thirty minutes before you need it, then combine with the krokan pieces.
(*The Roald Dahl Cookbook*)

This great feast would be interrupted by a small speech of welcome from my grandfather, and the grown-ups would raise their long-stemmed wine glasses and say 'skaal' many times throughout the meal.

When the guzzling was over, those who were considered old enough were given small glasses of home-made liqueur, a colourless but fiery drink that smelled of mulberries. The glasses were raised again and again, and the 'skaaling' seemed to go on for ever. In Norway, you may select any individual around the table and skaal him or her in a small private ceremony. You first lift your glass high and call out the name. 'Bestemama!' you say. 'Skaal, Bestemama!'

She will then lift her own glass and hold it up high. At the same time your own eyes meet hers, and you *must* keep looking deep into her eyes as you sip your drink. After you have both done this, you raise your glasses high up again in a sort of silent final salute, and only then does each person look away and set down his glass. It is a serious and solemn ceremony, and as a rule on formal occasions everyone skaals everyone else round the table once. If there are, for example, ten people present and you are one of them, you will skaal your nine companions once each individually, and you yourself will also receive nine separate skaals at different times during the meal – eighteen in all. That's how they work it in polite society over there, at least they used to in the old days, and quite a business it was. By the time I was ten, I would be permitted to take part in these ceremonies, and I always finished up as tipsy as a lord.

Skaal or skål is pronounced 'skawl' and means 'cheers!' The tradition of toasting each and every person dates back to Viking times, when fearsome warriors raised horns filled to the brim with beer.

Bestemama and Bestepapa (and Astri)

The magic island

THE HARBOUR
DRÖBAK.

THE BATHING HOUSE
MENS   LADIES.

The next morning, everyone got up early and eager to continue the journey. There was another full day's travelling to be done before we reached our final destination, most of it by boat. So after a rapid breakfast, our cavalcade left the Grand Hotel in three more taxis and headed for Oslo docks. There we went on board a small coastal steamer, and Nanny was heard to say, 'I'm sure it leaks! We shall all be food for the fishes before the day is out!' Then she would disappear below for the rest of the trip.

We loved this part of the journey. The splendid little vessel with its single tall funnel would move out into

Fra Havna. Rössesund   Eneret A. Mathisen fotograf Tönsberg

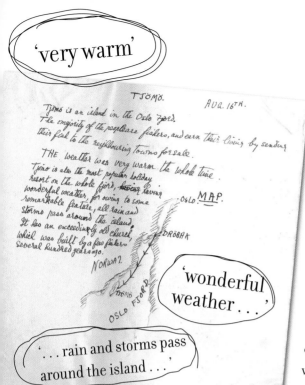

'very warm'

TJÖMÖ.   AUG. 16TH.

Tjömö is an island in the Oslo fjord.
The majority of the population are fishers, and earn their living by sending
their fish to the neighbouring towns for sale.

THE weather was very warm the whole time.

Tjömö is also the most popular holiday
resort on the whole fjord, having
wonderful weather, for owing to some
remarkable feature, all rain and
storms pass around the island.
It has an exceedingly old church
which was built by a few fishers
several hundred years ago.

OSLO MAP.

DRÖBAK

NORWAY.

TJÖMÖ OSLO FJORD.

'wonderful
weather . . .'

'. . . rain and storms pass
around the island . . .'

Roald's Norway
scrapbook about
Tjöme, the island
where the Dahl
family spent idyllic
summers.

the calm waters of the fjord and proceed at a leisurely pace along the coast, stopping every hour or so at a small wooden jetty where a group of villagers and summer people would be waiting to welcome friends or to collect parcels and mail. Unless you have sailed down the Oslofjord like this yourself on a tranquil summer's day, you cannot imagine what it is like. It is impossible to describe the sensation of absolute peace and beauty that surrounds you. The boat weaves in and out between countless tiny islands, some with small brightly painted wooden houses on them, but many with not a house or a tree on the bare rocks. These granite rocks are so smooth that you can lie and sun yourself on them in your bathing-costume without putting a towel underneath. We would see long-legged girls and tall boys basking on the rocks of the islands. There are no sandy beaches on the fjord. The rocks go straight down to the water's edge and the water is immediately deep. As a result, Norwegian children all learn to swim when they are very young because if you can't swim it is difficult to find a place to bathe.

Sometimes when our little vessel slipped between two small islands, the channel was so narrow we could almost touch the rocks on either side. We would pass row-boats and canoes with flaxen-haired children in them, their skins browned by the sun, and we would wave to them and watch their tiny boats rocking violently in the swell that our larger ship left behind.

Late in the afternoon, we would come finally to the end of the journey, the island of Tjöme. This was where our mother always took us. Heaven knows how she found it, but to us it was the greatest place on earth. About two hundred yards from the jetty, along a narrow dusty road, stood a simple wooden hotel painted white. It was run by an elderly couple whose faces I still remember vividly, and every year they welcomed us like old friends. Everything about the hotel was extremely primitive, except the dining-room. The walls, the ceiling and the floor of our bedrooms were made of plain unvarnished pine planks. There was a washbasin and a jug of cold water in each of them. The lavatories were in a rickety wooden outhouse at the back of the hotel and each cubicle contained nothing more than a round hole cut in a piece of wood. You sat on the hole and what you did there dropped into a pit ten feet below. If you looked down the hole, you would often see rats scurrying about in the gloom. All this we took for granted.

Havna Hotel, Tjöme.

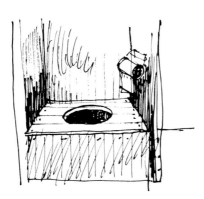

Breakfast was the best meal of the day in our hotel, and it was all laid out on a huge table in the middle of the dining-room from which you helped yourself. There were maybe fifty different dishes to choose from on that table. There were large jugs of milk, which all Norwegian children drink at every meal.

There were plates of cold beef, veal, ham and pork. There was cold boiled mackerel submerged in aspic. There were spiced and pickled herring fillets, sardines, smoked eels and cod's roe. There was a large bowl piled high with hot boiled eggs. There were cold omelettes with chopped ham in them, and cold chicken and hot coffee for the grown-ups, and hot crisp rolls baked in the hotel kitchen, which we ate with butter and cranberry jam. There were stewed apricots and five or six different cheeses including of course the ever-present gjetost, that tall brown rather sweet Norwegian goat's cheese which you find on just about every table in the land.

After breakfast, we collected our bathing things and the whole party, all ten of us, would pile into our boat.

Everyone has some sort of a boat in Norway. Nobody sits around in front of the hotel. Nor does anyone sit on the beach because there aren't any beaches to sit on. In the early days, we had only a row-boat, but a very fine one it was. It carried all of us easily, with places for two rowers. My mother took one pair of oars and my fairly ancient half-brother took the other, and off we would go.

My mother and the half-brother (he was somewhere around eighteen then) were expert rowers. They kept in perfect time and the oars went *click-click, click-click* in their wooden rowlocks, and the rowers never paused once during the long forty-minute journey. The rest of us sat in the boat trailing our fingers in the clear water and looking for jellyfish. We skimmed across the sound and went whizzing through narrow channels with rocky islands on either side, heading as always for a very secret tiny patch of sand on a distant island that only we knew about. In the early days we needed a place like this where we could paddle and play about because my youngest sister was only one, the next sister was three and I was four.

Not only was **Louis Dahl** an expert rower but, by accident, he also gave his half-brother Roald an idea for the name of the world's most famous chocolate-maker. Had Louis not invented a special boomerang – called a **Skilly Wonka** – then Roald may have ended up calling **Willy Wonka** something entirely different.

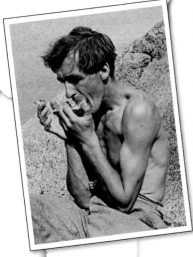

Louis Dahl.

The rocks and the deep water were no good to us.

Every day, for several summers, that tiny secret sand-patch on that tiny secret island was our regular destination. We would stay there for three or four hours, messing about in the water and in the rockpools and getting extraordinarily sunburnt.

THE BEACH.

A VIKINGS GRAVE.

Roald Dahl's Norway scrapbook about other islands.

Me, Alfhild, Else Norway 1924

In later years, when we were all a little older and could swim, the daily routine became different. By then, my mother had acquired a motor-boat, a small and not very seaworthy white wooden vessel which sat far too low in the water and was powered by an unreliable one-cylinder engine. The fairly ancient half-brother was the only one who could make the engine go at all. It was extremely difficult to start, and he always had to unscrew the sparking-plug and pour petrol into the cylinder. Then he swung a flywheel round and round, and with a bit of luck, after a lot of coughing and spluttering, the thing would finally get going.

This boat was known to the family as 'The Hard Black Stinker'.

When we first acquired the motor-boat, my youngest sister was four and I was seven, and by then all of us had learnt to swim. The exciting new boat made it possible for us to go much farther afield, and every day we would travel far out into the fjord, hunting for a different island. There were hundreds of them to choose from. Some were very small, no more than thirty yards long. Others were quite large, maybe half a mile in length. It was wonderful to have such a choice of places, and it was terrific fun to explore each island before we went swimming off the rocks. There were the wooden skeletons of shipwrecked boats on those islands, and big white bones (were they human bones?), and wild raspberries, and mussels clinging to the rocks, and some of the islands had shaggy long-haired goats on them, and even sheep.

Postcard of islands off Tjöme.

Now and again, when we were out in the open water beyond the chain of islands, the sea became very rough, and that was when my mother enjoyed herself most. Nobody, not even the tiny children, bothered with lifebelts in those days. We would cling to the sides of our funny little white motor-boat, driving through mountainous white-capped waves and getting drenched to the skin, while my mother calmly handled the tiller. There were times, I promise you, when the waves were so high that as we slid down into a trough the whole world disappeared from sight. Then up and up the little boat would climb, standing almost vertically on its tail, until we reached the crest of the next wave, and then it was like being on top of a foaming mountain. It requires great skill to handle a small boat in seas like these. The thing can easily capsize or be swamped if the bows do not meet the great combing breakers at just the right angle. But my mother knew exactly how to do it, and we were never afraid. We loved every minute of it, all of us except for our long-suffering Nanny, who would bury her face in her hands and call aloud upon the Lord to save her soul.

The Mussel Collectors
– the Dahl children and their cousins. (Roald Dahl is second from right.)

In the early evenings we nearly always went out fishing. We collected mussels from the rocks for bait, then we got into either the row-boat or the motor-boat and pushed off to drop anchor later in some likely spot. The water was very deep and often we had to let out two hundred feet of line before we touched bottom. We would sit silent and tense, waiting for a bite, and it always amazed me how even a little nibble at the end of that long line would be transmitted to one's fingers. 'A bite!' someone would shout, jerking the line. 'I've got him! It's a big one! It's a whopper!' And then came the thrill of hauling in the line hand over hand and peering over the side into the clear water to see how big the fish really was as he

Fishing on the Oslofjord.

neared the surface. Cod, whiting, haddock and mackerel, we caught them all and bore them back triumphantly to the hotel kitchen where the cheery fat woman who did the cooking promised to get them ready for our supper.

I tell you, my friends, those were the days.

A visit to the doctor

I have only one unpleasant memory of the summer holidays in Norway. We were in the grandparents' house in Oslo and my mother said to me, 'We are going to the doctor this afternoon. He wants to look at your nose and mouth.'

I think I was eight at the time. 'What's wrong with my nose and mouth?' I asked.

'Nothing much,' my mother said. 'But I think you've got adenoids.'

'What are *they*?' I asked her.

'Don't worry about it,' she said. 'It's nothing.'

I held my mother's hand as we walked to the doctor's house. It took us about half an hour. There was a kind of dentist's chair in the surgery and I was lifted into it. The doctor had a round mirror strapped to his forehead and he peered up my nose and into my mouth. He then took my mother aside and they held a whispered conversation. I saw my mother looking rather grim, but she nodded.

The doctor now put some water to boil in an aluminium mug over a gas flame, and into the boiling water he placed a long thin shiny steel instrument. I sat there watching the steam coming off the boiling water. I was not in the least apprehensive. I was too young to realize that something out of the ordinary was going to happen.

Then a nurse dressed in white came in. She was carrying a

Roald Dahl aged eight.

red rubber apron and a curved white enamel bowl. She put the apron over the front of my body and tied it around my neck. It was far too big. Then she held the enamel bowl under my chin. The curve of the bowl fitted perfectly against the curve of my chest.

The doctor was bending over me. In his hand he held that long shiny steel instrument. He held it right in front of my face, and to this day I can still describe it perfectly. It was about the thickness and length of a pencil, and like most pencils it had a lot of sides to it. Toward the end, the metal became much thinner, and at the very end of the thin bit of metal there was a tiny blade set at an angle. The blade wasn't more than a centimetre long, very small, very sharp and very shiny.

'Open your mouth,' the doctor said, speaking Norwegian.

Roald Dahl had **bad teeth** from quite a young age – probably due to having a **sweet tooth**. By the time he was in his **twenties** he had to wear **false teeth**!

I refused. I thought he was going to do something to my teeth, and everything anyone had ever done to my teeth had been painful.

'It won't take two seconds,' the doctor said. He spoke gently, and I was seduced by his voice. Like an ass, I opened my mouth.

The tiny blade flashed in the bright light and disappeared into my mouth. It went high up into the roof of my mouth, and the hand that held the blade gave four or five very quick little twists and the next moment, out of my mouth into the basin came tumbling a whole mass of flesh and blood.

I was too shocked and outraged to do anything but yelp. I was horrified by the huge red lumps that had fallen out of my mouth into the white basin and my first thought was that the doctor had cut out the whole of the middle of my head.

'Those were your adenoids,' I heard the doctor saying.

I sat there gasping. The roof of my mouth seemed to be on fire. I grabbed my mother's hand and held on to it tight. I couldn't believe that anyone would do this to me.

'Stay where you are,' the doctor said. 'You'll be all right in a minute.'

Blood was still coming out of my mouth and dripping into the basin the nurse was holding. 'Spit it all out,' she said, 'there's a good boy.'

'You'll be able to breathe much better through your nose after this,' the doctor said.

The nurse wiped my lips and washed my face with a wet flannel. Then they lifted me out of the chair and stood me on my feet. I felt a bit groggy.

'We'll get you home,' my mother said, taking my hand. Down the stairs we went and on to the street. We started walking. I said *walking*. No trolley-car or taxi. We walked the full half-hour journey back to my grandparents' house, and when we arrived at last, I can remember as clearly as anything my grandmother saying, 'Let him sit down in that chair and

Adenoids are small lumps of tissue found at the back of the throat, just above the tonsils. They help fight infection and protect the body from bacteria and viruses. But did you know that only children have adenoids? They begin to shrink when a child is about seven years old and will have completely vanished by the time they're grown up. By then, the body has developed much more effective ways of battling infections and viruses.

It wasn't the last time poor Roald Dahl had to visit a **doctor**. He had no less than **six** operations on his spine, **two** hip replacements and an emergency operation for a **burst appendix**. But despite these – and many more – medical problems, he said he would have wanted to be a doctor if he had not been a writer.

rest for a while. After all, he's had an operation.'

Someone placed a chair for me beside my grandmother's armchair, and I sat down. My grandmother reached over and covered one of my hands in both of hers. 'That won't be the last time you'll go to a doctor in your life,' she said. 'And with a bit of luck, they won't do you too much harm.'

That was in 1924, and taking out a child's adenoids, and often the tonsils as well, without any anaesthetic was common practice in those days. I wonder, though, what you would think if some doctor did that to you today.

The Last Lap

For four weeks every summer we stayed in that lovely white hotel on the island of Tjöme. But that was never the whole of the holiday. Our indefatigable mother was not nearly finished yet. Her plan was always that we should have those four weeks by the sea during August and then, as the weather began to get cooler, we would all move up into the mountains for another ten days before finally returning home.

After ten days in our mountain hotel, we took the train, not back to Oslo, but onward to Bergen on the west coast, and from there we caught a boat to Newcastle. Then Newcastle to London and London to home.

I don't think we knew how lucky we were to have a holiday like that every summer of our growing-up lives. I don't think we knew either how lucky we were to have a mother who gave us such a lovely time every year.

TYNE BRIDGE.

GREY STREET.

1 36 (one thirty six) please meet me. This is
the longest letter I have written to you this term.

LAST
SUND ... ER.

...ON-SUPER-MARE.

...Form V. Number of Boys 16. Average Age 13. Place in Form 5.

Michaelmas Term, 1928.

SUBJECT	Order	REMARKS	Master
SCRIPTURE			
HISTORY	4	Good.	
ENGLISH GRAMMAR	6	Very fair.	
ENGLISH COMPOSITION / ENGLISH LITERATURE	3,	Steadily improving. Takes great pains with his essays and are much improved.	A.J.H.F.
GENERAL KNOWLEDGE		Excellent	A.J.H.F.
GEOGRAPHY			
LATIN	4	Very good. 1st in Term.	C.L.B.
GREEK or GERMAN	11.	Not a strong subject, though he works hard as a rule.	
ARITHMETIC			
ALGEBRA	3	Is making good progress	J.H.C.
GEOMETRY	2		S.L.
FRENCH	4		
MUSIC	6	Keen. Lacks confidence in himself.	J.H.C.
BOXING		Is making good progress, but is rather stiff and slow on his feet.	A.F.
GAMES		A very effective outside right, who, though not very fast, generally gets there. His centring is excellent.	V.R.C.
SECTION		Was made an Excellent Captain and is doing v. well.	S.L.
HOUSE		Considerably improved. More reliable.	
GENERAL		He is making steady progress. Above the standard of his age.	V.R.C.

Boys return on Monday, Jan 21st 1929.

A. J. H. Francis

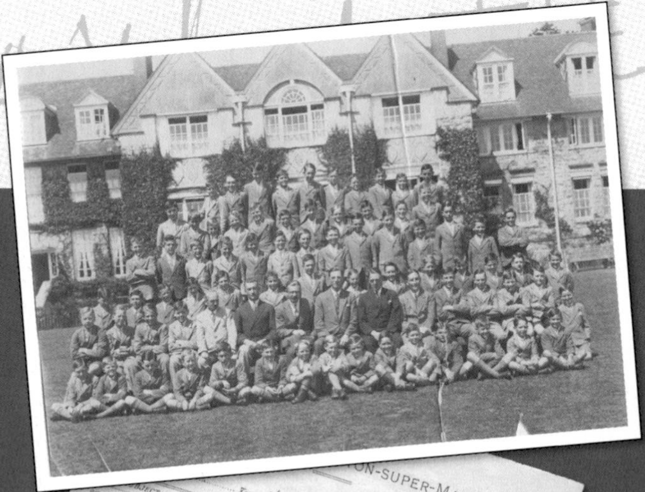

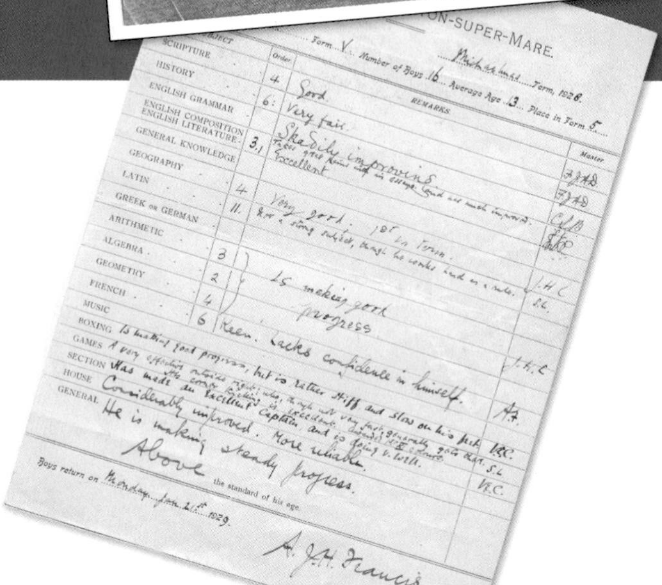

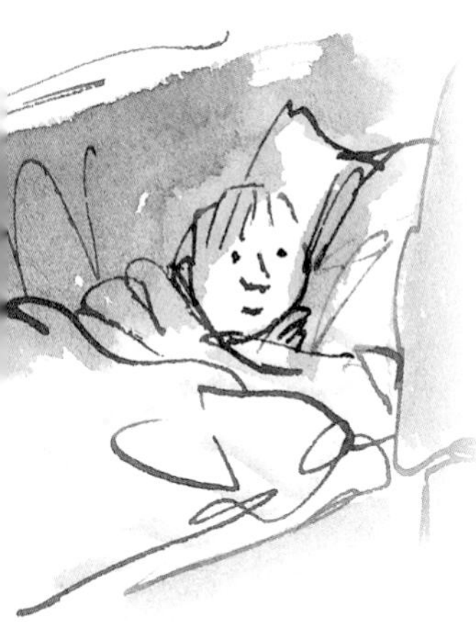

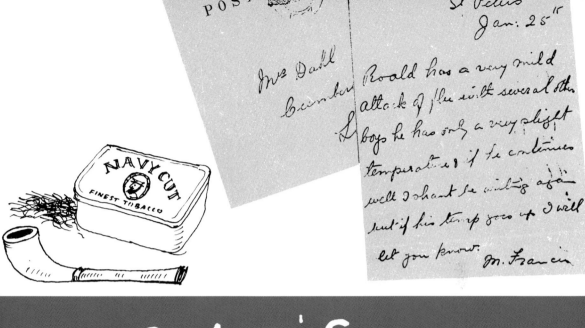

St Peters
Jan: 25th

Mrs Dahl
Cumber...

Roald has a very mild attack of flue with several other boys he has only a very slight temperature & if he continues well I shant be writing again but if his temp goes up I will let you know.
M. Francis

St Peter's 1925-29 (age 9-13)

St Peters........School
Date of Issue...July 8th...1925
STAR No.....8...Issued this Term by...RHB
NAME (of pupil)...Dahl
is sent up with a "STAR" won thus :—
¼ for Arithmetic.........by :— RHB
¼ for Latin.........by :— S.L.
¼ for Literature.........by :— J.H.C
¼ for Algebra.........by...Bay.

The recipient of this STAR must carefully and neatly fill up this Column in Ink before showing it up or it will be refused.
This is my STAR No...1...won this Term.
Last Term, including any cancelled, I won...12...STARS.
This Term I have got, up to this date...1½...
This is my...1st...STRIPES.
Term in the School.
The record after my name at the end of last Term was...
Signature of recipient:...
Date of completion...

6925-DK75

St Peters uniform

Jack Hobbs
Cumberland Lodge Llandaff

Duckworth Butterflies my house
St. Peters
me in front row

Asta Else Alfhild me
Cardiff 1927

The boys at St Peter's School were divided into two houses, called 'Duckworth' and 'Crawford'.

First day

In September 1925, when I was just nine, I set out on the first great adventure of my life – boarding-school. My mother had chosen for me a Prep School in a part of England which was as near as it could possibly be to our home in South Wales, and it was called St Peter's. The full postal address was St Peter's School, Weston-super-Mare, Somerset.

Weston-super-Mare.

Weston-super-Mare is a slightly seedy seaside resort with a vast sandy beach, a tremendous long pier, an esplanade running along the sea-front, a clutter of hotels and boarding-houses, and about ten thousand little shops selling buckets and spades and sticks of rock and ice-creams. It lies almost directly across the Bristol Channel from Cardiff, and on a clear day you can stand on the esplanade at Weston and look across the fifteen or so miles of water and see the coast of Wales lying pale and milky on the horizon.

In those days the easiest way to travel from Cardiff to Weston-super-Mare was by boat. Those boats were beautiful. They were paddle-steamers, with gigantic swishing paddle-wheels on their flanks, and the wheels made the most terrific noise as they sloshed and churned through the water.

Now the easiest way to travel from Cardiff to Weston-super-Mare is over the magnificent Severn Bridge. Opened by Queen Elizabeth II in 1966, it was forty-one years too late for Roald Dahl.

On the first day of my first term I set out by taxi in the afternoon with my mother to catch the paddle-steamer from Cardiff Docks to Weston-super-Mare. Every piece of clothing I wore was brand new and had my name on it. I wore black shoes, grey woollen stockings with blue turnovers, grey flannel shorts, a grey shirt, a red tie, a grey flannel blazer with the blue school crest on the breast pocket and a grey school cap with the same crest just above the peak. Into the taxi that was taking us to the docks went my brand new trunk and my brand new tuck-box, and both had R. DAHL painted on them in black.

A **preparatory school** – **prep school** for short – is a fee-paying school that **prepares** children for public school. Roald Dahl went to **prep** school between the ages of nine and thirteen. Nothing had **prepared** him for this.

A tuck-box is a small pinewood trunk which is very strongly made, and no boy has ever gone as a boarder to an English Prep School without one. It is his own secret store-house, as secret as a lady's handbag, and there is an unwritten law that no other boy, no teacher, not even the Headmaster himself has the right to pry into the contents of your tuck-box. The owner has the key in his pocket and that is where it stays. At St Peter's, the tuck-boxes were ranged shoulder to shoulder all around the four walls of the changing-room and your own tuck-box stood directly below the peg on which you hung your games clothes. A tuck-box, as the name implies, is a box in which you store your tuck. At Prep School in those days, a parcel of tuck was sent once a week by anxious mothers to their ravenous little sons, and an average tuck-box would probably contain, at almost any time, half a home-made currant cake, a packet of squashed-fly biscuits, a couple of oranges, an apple, a banana, a pot of strawberry jam or Marmite, a bar of chocolate, a bag of Liquorice Allsorts and a tin of Bassett's lemonade powder. An English school in those days was purely a money-making business owned and operated by the Headmaster. It suited him, therefore, to give the boys as little food as possible himself and to encourage the parents in various cunning ways to feed their offspring by parcel-post from home.

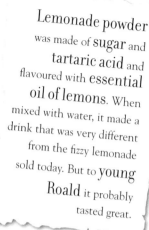

Lemonade powder was made of sugar and tartaric acid and flavoured with essential oil of lemons. When mixed with water, it made a drink that was very different from the fizzy lemonade sold today. But to young Roald it probably tasted great.

'By all means, my dear Mrs Dahl, *do* send your boy some little treats now and again,' he would say. 'Perhaps a few oranges and apples once a week' – fruit was very expensive – 'and a nice currant cake, a *large* currant cake perhaps because small boys have large appetites, do they not, ha-ha-ha . . . Yes, yes, as *often* as you like. *More* than once a week if you wish . . . *Of course* he'll be getting plenty of good food here, the best there is, but it never tastes *quite* the same as home cooking, does it? I'm sure you wouldn't want him to be the only one who doesn't get a lovely parcel from home every week.'

A Mexican jumping bean is a very special type of seed, found in Mexico. The egg of a small moth is laid inside the bean and when the moth's larva moves, the bean appears to jump. They were in great demand in the 1930s.

As well as tuck, a tuck-box would also contain all manner of treasures such as a magnet, a pocket-knife, a compass, a ball of string, a clockwork racing-car, half a dozen lead soldiers, a box of conjuring-tricks, some tiddly-winks, a Mexican jumping bean, a catapult, some foreign stamps, a couple of stink-bombs, and I remember one boy called Arkle who drilled an airhole in the lid of his tuck-box and kept a pet frog in there which he fed on slugs.

So off we set, my mother and I and my trunk and my tuck-box, and we boarded the paddle-steamer and went swooshing across the Bristol Channel in a shower of spray. I liked that part of it, but I began to grow apprehensive as I disembarked on to the pier at Weston-super-Mare and watched my trunk and tuck-box being loaded into an English taxi which would drive us to St Peter's. I had absolutely no idea what was in store for me. I had never spent a single night away from our large family before.

St Peter's was on a hill above the town. It was a long three-storeyed stone building that looked rather like a private lunatic asylum, and in front of it lay the playing-fields with their three football pitches. One-third of the building was reserved for the Headmaster and his family. The rest of it housed the boys, about one hundred and fifty of them altogether, if I remember rightly.

As we got out of the taxi, I saw the whole driveway abustle with small boys and their parents and their trunks and their tuck-boxes, and a man I took to be the Headmaster was swimming around among them shaking everybody by the hand.

I have already told you that *all* Headmasters are giants, and this one was no exception. He advanced upon my mother and shook her by the hand, then he shook me by the hand and as he did so he gave me the kind of flashing

the Loony Bin!

grin a shark might give to a small fish just before he gobbles it up. One of his front teeth, I noticed, was edged all the way round with gold, and his hair was slicked down with so much hair-cream that it glistened like butter.

'Right,' he said to me. 'Off you go and report to the Matron.' And to my mother he said briskly, 'Goodbye, Mrs Dahl. I shouldn't linger if I were you. We'll look after him.'

My mother got the message. She kissed me on the cheek and said goodbye and climbed right back into the taxi.

The Headmaster moved away to another group and I was left standing there beside my brand new trunk and my brand new tuck-box. I began to cry.

There are **seventy-three boys** in this school photo (go on, count them!) taken at St Peter's in about 1929.

Writing home

At St Peter's, Sunday morning was letter-writing time. At nine o'clock the whole school had to go to their desks and spend one hour writing a letter home to their parents. At ten-fifteen we put on our caps and coats and formed up outside the school in a long crocodile and marched a couple of miles down into Weston-super-Mare for church, and we didn't get back until lunchtime. Church-going never became a habit with me. Letter-writing did.

Here is the very first letter I wrote home from St Peter's.

Dear Mama   23rd Spt
    I am having a lovely time here.
We play foot ball every day here. The beds
beds have no springs. Will you send my
stamp album, and quite a lot of swops.
The masters are very nice. I've
got all my clothes now, and a belt,
and, tie, and a school Jersey.
        love from
        Boy

Roald Dahl was known to his family as 'Boy'. As you can see from his letters, when he first went away to school he even signed himself 'Boy'. This lasted for about a term: after that, all his letters are signed 'love from Roald'.

From that very first Sunday at St Peter's until the day my mother died thirty-two years later, I wrote to her once a week, sometimes more often, whenever I was away from home. I wrote to her every week from St Peter's (I had to), and every week from my next school, Repton, and every week from Dar es Salaam in East Africa, where I went on my first job after leaving school, and then every week during the war from Kenya and Iraq and Egypt when I was flying with the RAF.

> ... Major Cottam is going to recite something caled "as you like it" To night. Plese could you send me some conkers as quick as you can, but ~~dorant~~ dont send To meny, ~~the~~ Just send them in a Tin and wrapit up in paper

My mother, for her part, kept every one of these letters, binding them carefully in neat bundles with green tape, but this was her own secret. She never told me she was doing it. In 1967, when she knew she was dying, I was in hospital in Oxford having a serious operation on my spine and I was unable to write to her. So she had a telephone specially installed beside her bed in order that she might have one last conversation with me. She didn't tell me she was dying nor did anyone else for that matter because I was in a fairly serious condition myself at the time. She simply asked me how I was and hoped I would get better soon and sent me her love. I had no idea that she would die the next day, but she knew all right and she wanted to reach out and speak to me for the last time.

Mama in 1964 when she was seventy-nine years old.

When I recovered and went home, I was given this vast collection of my letters, all so neatly bound with green tape, more than six hundred of them altogether, dating from 1925 to 1945, each one in its original envelope with the old stamps still on them. I am awfully lucky to have something like this to refer to in my old age.

Only one term's letters are missing: **September – December 1928**. The Dahl family home was damaged by **bombing in 1940** so perhaps it's even more amazing that any letters survived at all! There are over **four hundred** of them altogether, and now they are all kept in Roald Dahl's archive, **the Roald Dahl Museum and Story Centre**, Great Missenden.

Jan 19ᵗʰ 1926

Dear Mama
I got to school all right. Please send my music book as quick as possible. Don't forget to tell Smiths to send Bubbles

Love from
Boy

POST CARD

Mrs Dahl
Cumberland Lodge
Llandaff
Nr Cardiff

Bubbles was a children's comic.

Letter-writing was a serious business at St Peter's. It was as much a lesson in spelling and punctuation as anything else because the Headmaster would patrol the classrooms all through the sessions, peering over our shoulders to read what

this is my Christmas wish list as far as I can see.
A mashie-niblick (which I have to close).
A decent book.
I can't think of any thing else: If you send me a catalogue I might be able to tell you.

A mashie-niblick is not a pre-war chocolate bar. It is a golf club used for hitting high shots.

we were writing and to point out our mistakes. But that, I am quite sure, was not the main reason for his interest. He was there to make sure that we said nothing horrid about his school.

There was no way, therefore, that we could ever complain to our parents about anything during term-time. If we thought the food was lousy or if we hated a certain master or if we had been thrashed for something we did not do, we never dared to say so in our letters. In fact, we often went the other way. In order to please that dangerous Headmaster who was leaning over our shoulders and reading what we had written, we would say splendid things about the school and go on about how lovely the masters were.

> *. A man called Mr*
> Nichell gave us a fine lecture 'last knight on (birds) he told us how owls owls eat mice they eat the hole mouse shin and all, and then all the shin and bones goes into a sort of little parcel in side him and he puts it on the ground, and those are called pellets, and he showed us some pictures of some witch he has found, and of lotes of other Birds.'

Roald Dahl was always fascinated by birds:

'We have a pair of swallows that have built their nest in exactly the same place on a wooden beam in the tool shed for the past six years, and it is amazing to me how they fly off thousands of miles to North Africa in the autumn with their young and then six months later they find their way back to the same tool shed at Gipsy House, Great Missenden, Bucks. It's a miracle and the brainiest ornithologists in the world still cannot explain how they do it.'
(My Year)

Mind you, the Headmaster was a clever fellow. He did not want our parents to think that those letters of ours were censored in this way, and therefore he never allowed us to correct a spelling mistake in the letter itself. If, for example, I had written . . . *last Tuesday knight we had a lecture* . . . , he would say:

'Don't you know how to spell night?'

'Y-yes, sir, k-n-i-g-h-t.'

'That's the other kind of knight, you idiot!'

'Which kind, sir? I . . . I don't understand.'

'The one in shining armour! The man on horseback! How do you spell Tuesday night?'

'I . . . I . . . I'm not quite sure, sir.'

'It's n-i-g-h-t, boy, n-i-g-h-t. Stay in and write it out for me fifty times this afternoon. No, no! Don't change it in the letter! You don't want to make it any messier than it is! It must go as you wrote it!'

Thus, the unsuspecting parents received in this subtle way the impression that your letter had never been seen or censored or corrected by anyone.

St Peter's
Weston-super-mare.

Jan. 27th 1928.

Dear Mama Thank you very much for the cake etc. I got the book the day before yesterday, quite a nice edition. How are 'the chicks'? hope they'll all live. By the way, you said she wouldn't get any.

More About Boy

St Peter's,
Weston-super-mare.
Feb 24th 1926.

Dear Alfhild
    We have got a craze for Baby tractors now, nearly every one is ordering them and Mrs Frances buys them for us, we have races and hill climing tests and see whose goes ¥ up the steepest hill, but they are very (pourful) We are having a matheh to day, we are

playing Clarénce ²school, I think they have got quite a good team but I hope we will win. I have nearly got three more quater-stars, another for Arithmetic, and one for Poetry and one for Writing, so that is my second one for Arithmetic.
    Love from

    BOY

RD 13/1/1/35.

Roald Dahl's spelling was quite dreadful when he was young.

St Peter's
Weston-super-mare.
March 24th 1926.

Dear Else
    I will soon be coming home, I am coming by train next Wedensday. There is a craze for darts and gliders, nearly every one has got one, I have got one topping one, it glides like any thig, a boy called Huntly-Wood made it for me, I have got five quater-

stars, I got one of them to day, it was for writing from Mr Francis. I think the French Play was very good, and very funny as well, I could not understand much of it, but I think every one liked it.
    Love from

    BOY

RD 13/1/1/44.

Oct. 13th 1929.

St. Peter's.

Weston-super-mare

Dear Mama

Thanks awfully for the Roller skates, they are topphole. Were they the largest pair? At full stretch they fit toppingly, but if my feet grow much more they wont fit. We skate on the yard; we had a toj fine time last night after tea; You see, the chaps who haven't got pairs, pull you. At one time I had eight chaps pulling me with a long rope, at a terrific lick, and, I sat down in the middle of it; my bottom is all blue now! We also have "trains". You get about ten chaps to pull, and with a long rope, and all the roller-skaters hang on to each other, and go around; but if one chap falls all the ones behind him come on top of him; the yard is

In the 1920s, 'topping' and 'tophole' meant the same as 'cool' today.

getting quite smooth now.

Last wednesday we played a school called "Clarence" and beat them in 3-1. So far we have played 3 matches and won them all; so far we have as good a term as the Rugger.

Last Sunday we had a lantern lecture on Lighthouses; the man, gave pictures of "The Wolf", "Eddigard" the Bishops Rock, and Longships at Landsend, all of which we saw last hols.

By the way, I had a birthday present from Marsali yesterday. It was a thing called a "Yoo Yah", which runs up and down on a string, but is very hard to work. It is very fascinating, but she confessed that it was bought at Woolworths; and she said that it was the craze there. I show you when I get home. Can you send me another tube of 'Genoo' toothpaste please.

Love from Roald.

'Rugger' is a nickname for 'rugby'.

Can you guess what this might be called now?

RD 13/1/5

This is **Matron**. Oops, sorry. No. It's actually Miss Trunchbull from *Matilda*. But it's very easy to get them **mixed up**.

The Matron

At St Peter's the ground floor was all classrooms. The first floor was all dormitories. On the dormitory floor the Matron ruled supreme. This was her territory. Hers was the only voice of authority up here, and even the eleven- and twelve-year-old boys were terrified of this female ogre, for she ruled with a rod of steel.

The Matron was a large fair-haired woman with a bosom. Her age was probably no more than twenty-eight but it made no difference whether she was twenty-eight or sixty-eight because to us a grown-up was a grown-up and all grown-ups were dangerous creatures at this school.

Once you had climbed to the top of the stairs and set foot on the dormitory floor, you were in the Matron's power, and the source of this power was the unseen but frightening figure of the Headmaster lurking down in the depths of his study below. At any time she liked, the Matron could send you down in your pyjamas and dressing-gown to report to this merciless giant, and whenever this happened you got caned on the spot. The Matron knew this and she relished the whole business.

She could move along that corridor like lightning, and when you least expected it, her head and her bosom would come popping through the dormitory doorway. 'Who threw that sponge?' the dreaded voice would call out. 'It was *you*, Perkins, was it not? Don't lie to me, Perkins! Don't argue

A **school matron** was in charge of domestic or medical arrangements. She supervised the pupils. At Roald Dahl's school, she terrified them too.

Roald Dahl described **Perkins** to his mother as 'my best friend'. He was a mean **conker player** too. Roald himself was a **connoisseur of conkers**:

'It is no good knocking down conkers in August. But in September, ah, yes, then they are a deep rich brown colour and shining as though they have been polished and that is the time to gather them by the bucketful.'
(My Year)

with me! I know perfectly well it was you! Now you can put your dressing-gown on and go downstairs and report to the Headmaster this instant!'

In slow motion and with immense reluctance, little Perkins, aged eight and a half, would get into his dressing-gown and slippers and disappear down the long corridor that led to the back stairs and the Headmaster's private quarters. And the Matron, as we all knew, would follow after him and stand at the top of the stairs listening with a funny look on her face for the *crack . . . crack . . . crack* of the cane that would soon be coming up from below. To me that noise always sounded as though the Headmaster was firing a pistol at the ceiling of his study.

Looking back on it now, there seems little doubt that the Matron disliked small boys very much indeed. She never smiled at us or said anything nice, and when for example the lint stuck to the cut on your kneecap, you were not allowed to take it off yourself bit by bit so that it didn't hurt. She would always whip it off with a flourish, muttering, 'Don't be such a ridiculous little baby!'

'We've got a new matron. Last term, one night in the washing room, having inspected a boy called Ford she kissed him and ~

On one occasion during my first term, I went down to the Matron's room to have some iodine put on a grazed knee and I didn't know you had to knock before you entered. I opened the door and walked right in, and there she was in the centre of the Sick Room floor locked in some kind of an embrace with the Latin master, Mr Victor Corrado. They flew apart as I entered and both their faces went suddenly crimson.

'How *dare* you come in without knocking!' the Matron shouted. 'Here I am trying to get something out of Mr Corrado's eye and in you burst and disturb the whole delicate operation!'

'I'm very sorry, Matron.'

'Go away and come back in five minutes!' she cried, and I shot out of the room like a bullet.

After 'lights out' the Matron would prowl the corridor like a panther trying to catch the sound of a whisper behind a dormitory door, and we soon learnt that her powers of hearing were so phenomenal that it was safer to keep quiet.

Once, after lights out, a brave boy called Wragg tiptoed out of our dormitory and sprinkled castor sugar all over the linoleum floor of the corridor. When Wragg returned and told us that the corridor had been successfully sugared from one end to the other, I began shivering with excitement. I lay there in the dark in my bed waiting and waiting for the Matron to go on the prowl. Nothing happened. Perhaps, I told myself, she is in her room taking another speck of dust out of Mr Victor Corrado's eye.

Suddenly, from far down the corridor came a resounding *crunch! Crunch crunch crunch* went the footsteps. It sounded as though a giant was walking on loose gravel.

Then we heard the high-pitched furious voice of the Matron in the distance. 'Who did this?' she was shrieking. 'How *dare* you do this!' She went crunching along the corridor flinging open all the dormitory doors and switching on all the lights. The intensity of her fury was frightening. 'Come along!' she cried out, marching with crunching steps up and down the corridor. 'Own up! I want the name of the filthy little boy who

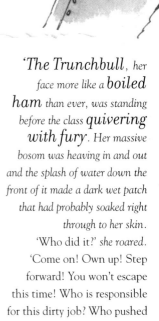

'The Trunchbull, her face more like a *boiled ham* than ever, was standing before the class *quivering with fury*. Her massive bosom was heaving in and out and the splash of water down the front of it made a dark wet patch that had probably soaked right through to her skin.
'Who did it?' she roared.
'Come on! Own up! Step forward! You won't escape this time! Who is responsible for this dirty job? Who pushed over this glass?'
Nobody answered. The whole room remained *silent as a tomb.*'
(Matilda)

put down the sugar! Own up immediately! Step forward! Confess!'

'Don't own up,' we whispered to Wragg. 'We won't give you away!'

Wragg kept quiet. I didn't blame him for that. Had he owned up, it was certain his fate would have been a terrible and a bloody one.

Soon the Headmaster was summoned from below. The Matron, with steam coming out of her nostrils, cried out to him for help, and now the whole school was herded into the long corridor, where we stood freezing in our pyjamas and bare feet while the culprit or culprits were ordered to step forward.

Nobody stepped forward.

I could see that the Headmaster was getting very angry indeed. His evening had been interrupted. Red splotches were appearing all over his face and flecks of spit were shooting out of his mouth as he talked.

'Very well!' he thundered. 'Every one of you will go at once and get the key to his tuck-box! Hand the keys to Matron, who will keep them for the rest of the term! And all parcels coming from home will be confiscated from now on! I will not tolerate this kind of behaviour!'

Roald Dahl's advice on frogs:

'Be nice to frogs, by the way. They are your friends in the garden. They eat the beastly slugs and never harm your flowers.'
(My Year)

We handed in our keys and throughout the remaining six weeks of the term we went very hungry. But all through those six weeks, Arkle continued to feed his frog with slugs through the hole in the lid of his tuck-box. Using an old teapot, he also poured water in through the hole every day to keep the creature moist and happy. I admired Arkle very much for looking after his frog so well. Although he himself was famished, he refused to let his frog go hungry. Ever since then I have tried to be kind to small animals.

Each dormitory had about twenty beds in it. These were smallish narrow beds ranged along the walls on either side. Down the centre of the dormitory stood the basins where you washed your hands and face and did your teeth, always with cold water which stood in large jugs on the floor. Once you had entered the dormitory, you were not allowed to leave it unless you were reporting to the Matron's room with some sickness or injury. Under each bed there was a white chamber-pot, and before getting into bed you were expected to kneel on the floor and empty your bladder into it. All around the dormitory, just before 'lights out', was heard the *tinkle-tinkle* of little boys peeing into their pots. Once you had done this and got into your bed, you were not allowed to get out of it again until next morning. There was, I believe, a lavatory somewhere along the corridor, but only an attack of acute diarrhoea would be accepted as an excuse for visiting it. A journey to the upstairs lavatory automatically classed you as a diarrhoea victim, and a dose of thick white liquid would immediately be forced down your throat by the Matron. This made you constipated for a week.

Things you might not know about **chamber-pots** ... They were usually ceramic. They often had a lid. They were also known as thunder pots, jordans, pos and **potties**.

Thanks for your letter. There are exactly 23 boys with the measles and all the other schools (boys) in here have got it. Hope Louis hasn't had anything else wrong

The first miserable homesick night at St Peter's, when I curled up in bed and the lights were put out, I could think of nothing but our house at home and my mother and my

sisters. Where were they? I asked myself. In which direction from where I was lying was Llandaff? I began to work it out and it wasn't difficult to do this because I had the Bristol Channel to help me. If I looked out of the dormitory window I could see the Channel itself, and the big city of Cardiff with Llandaff alongside it lay almost directly across the water but slightly to the north. Therefore, if I turned towards the window I would be facing home. I wriggled round in my bed and faced my home and my family.

From then on, during all the time I was at St Peter's, I never went to sleep with my back to my family. Different beds in different dormitories required the working out of new directions, but the Bristol Channel was always my guide and I was always able to draw an imaginary line from my bed to our house over in Wales. Never once did I go to sleep looking away from my family. It was a great comfort to do this.

As the crow flies, Roald Dahl's school was only 15 miles from his home in Llandaff. But it must have seemed much further away to a homesick boy.

Do you know that a chap called Ford has got double Pneumonia on top of measles!!!!!! we've all got to be like mice going up to bed.

There was a boy in our dormitory during my first term called Tweedie, who one night started snoring soon after he had gone to sleep.

'Who's that talking?' cried the Matron, bursting in. My own bed was close to the door, and I remember looking up at her from my pillow and seeing her standing there silhouetted against the light from the corridor and thinking how truly frightening she looked. I think it was her enormous bosom that scared me most of all. My eyes were riveted to it, and to me it was like a battering-ram or the bows of an icebreaker or maybe a couple of high-explosive bombs.

'Own up!' she cried. 'Who was talking?'

We lay there in silence. Then Tweedie, who was lying fast asleep on his back with his mouth open, gave another snore.

The Matron stared at Tweedie. 'Snoring is a disgusting habit,' she said. 'Only the lower classes do it. We shall have to teach him a lesson.'

She didn't switch on the light, but she advanced into the room and picked up a cake of soap from the nearest basin. The bare electric bulb in the corridor illuminated the whole dormitory in a pale creamy glow.

None of us dared to sit up in bed, but all eyes were on the Matron now, watching to see what she was going to do next. She always had a pair of scissors hanging by a white tape from her waist, and with this she began shaving thin slivers of soap into the palm of one hand. Then she went over to where the wretched Tweedie lay and very carefully she dropped these little soap-flakes into his open mouth. She had a whole handful of them and I thought she was never going to stop.

What on earth is going to happen? I wondered. Would Tweedie choke? Would he strangle? Might his throat get blocked up completely? Was she going to kill him?

The Matron stepped back a couple of paces and folded her arms across, or rather underneath, her massive chest.

Nothing happened. Tweedie kept right on snoring.

Then suddenly he began to gurgle and white bubbles appeared around his lips. The bubbles grew and grew until in the end his whole face seemed to be smothered in a bubbly foaming white soapy froth. It was a horrific sight. Then all at once, Tweedie gave a great cough and a splutter and he sat up very fast and began clawing at his face with his hands. 'Oh!' he stuttered. 'Oh! Oh! Oh! Oh no! Wh-wh-what's happening? Wh-wh-what's on my face? Somebody help me!'

The Matron threw him a face flannel and said, 'Wipe it off, Tweedie. And don't ever let me hear you snoring again. Hasn't anyone ever taught you not to go to sleep on your back?'

With that she marched out of the dormitory and slammed the door.

Reread the letter extracts throughout this chapter and you'll find out about Ford, who sadly died of **double pneumonia** after having had **measles** during an epidemic at the school in **February 1928**. Ford was **nine years old** when he died and had been at the school for less than a year.

very bad, he got better on Friday but has again got very ill. Ford is still P.S. We have just been informed that poor little Ford died early this morning.

Homesickness

I was homesick during the whole of my first term at St Peter's. Homesickness is a bit like seasickness. You don't know how awful it is till you get it, and when you do, it hits you right in the top of the stomach and you want to die. The only comfort is that both homesickness and seasickness are instantly curable. The first goes away the moment you walk out of the school grounds and the second is forgotten as soon as the ship enters port.

I was so devastatingly homesick during my first two weeks that I set about devising a stunt for getting myself sent back home, even if it were only a few days. My idea was that I should all of a sudden develop an attack of acute appendicitis.

You will probably think it silly that a nine-year-old boy should imagine he could get away with a trick like that, but I had sound reasons for trying it on. Only a

Never cry wolf.
Much later Roald Dahl really did have **appendicitis** in **1945**. He managed to get himself to hospital to have it removed in an **emergency operation**, but as he was living in the USA at the time he had to write to his mother afterwards to tell her about it!

I had two helpings also a dessert, a sort of strawberry Tart so that when I got a Tum Tummy ache at once afterwards I just thought that I had made a ~~my~~ of myself especially as the pain was high up in the Solar plexus. Well, I played one game of backgammon with Mrs Pearson then the Tummy-ache was pretty uncomfortable so I went home. I went to bed and was sick and lost a Cordell Hull down the lavatory, then I was sick again

The **appendix** is a tube in the abdomen. It leads nowhere and does nothing. But **appendicitis** – when the appendix becomes inflamed – is no joke. If left untreated, it can be deadly.

month before, my ancient half-sister, who was twelve years older than me, had actually *had* appendicitis, and for several days before her operation I was able to observe her behaviour at close quarters. I noticed that the thing she complained about most was a severe pain down in the lower right side of her tummy. As well as this, she kept being sick and refused to eat and ran a temperature.

You might, by the way, be interested to know that this sister had her appendix removed not in a fine hospital operating-room full of bright lights and gowned nurses but on our own nursery table at home by the local doctor and his anaesthetist. In those days it was fairly common practice for a doctor to

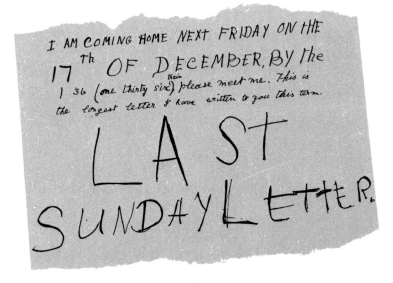

I AM COMING HOME NEXT FRIDAY ON THE 17th OF DECEMBER, BY the 1 36 (one thirty six) train please meet me. This is the longest letter I have written to you this term. LAST SUNDAY LETTER.

arrive at your own house with a bag of instruments, then drape a sterile sheet over the most convenient table and get on with it. On this occasion, I can remember lurking in the corridor outside the nursery while the operation was going on. My other sisters were with me, and we stood there spellbound, listening

to the soft medical murmurs coming from behind the locked door and picturing the patient with her stomach sliced open like a lump of beef. We could even smell the sickly fumes of ether filtering through the crack under the door.

The next day, we were allowed to inspect the appendix itself in a glass bottle. It was a longish black wormy-looking thing, and I said, 'Do *I* have one of those inside me, Nanny?'

'Everybody has one,' Nanny answered.

'What's it for?' I asked her.

'God works in his mysterious ways,' she said, which was her stock reply whenever she didn't know the answer.

'What makes it go bad?' I asked her.

'Toothbrush bristles,' she answered, this time with no hesitation at all.

'*Toothbrush* bristles?' I cried. 'How can *toothbrush* bristles make your appendix go bad?'

Nanny, who in my eyes was filled with more wisdom than Solomon, replied, 'Whenever a bristle comes out of your toothbrush and you swallow it, it sticks in your appendix and turns it rotten. In the war,' she went on, 'the German spies used to sneak boxloads of loose-bristled toothbrushes into our shops and millions of our soldiers got appendicitis.'

Did **Nanny's white lies** inspire Roald Dahl to come up with his own fantastic stories . . . ?

'Tell me what else to look out for in a witch?' I said. 'The eyes,' my grandmother said. 'Look carefully at the eyes, because the eyes of a REAL WITCH are different from yours and mine. Look in the middle of each eye where there is normally a little black dot. If she is a witch, the black dot will keep changing colour, and you will see fire and you will see ice dancing right in the very centre of the coloured dot. It will send shivers running all over your skin.'
(The Witches)

'When Bruce Bogtrotter had eaten his way through half of the entire enormous cake, he paused for just a couple of seconds and took several deep breaths.

The Trunchbull stood with hands on hips, glaring at him. 'Get on with it!' she shouted. 'Eat it up!'

Suddenly the boy let out a gigantic belch.'
(Matilda)

'Honestly, Nanny?' I cried. 'Is that honestly true?'

'I never lie to you, child,' she answered. 'So let that be a lesson to you never to use an old toothbrush.'

For years after that, I used to get nervous whenever I found a toothbrush bristle on my tongue.

As I went upstairs and knocked on the brown door after breakfast, I didn't even feel frightened of the Matron.

'Come in!' boomed the voice.

I entered the room clutching my stomach on the right-hand side and staggering pathetically.

'What's the matter with you?' the Matron shouted, and the sheer force of her voice caused that massive bosom to quiver like a gigantic blancmange.

'It hurts, Matron,' I moaned. 'Oh, it hurts so much! Just here!'

'You've been over-eating!' she barked. 'What do you expect if you guzzle currant cake all day long!'

'I haven't eaten a thing for days,' I lied. 'I *couldn't* eat, Matron! I simply *couldn't*!'

'Get on the bed and lower your trousers,' she ordered.

I lay on the bed and she began prodding my tummy violently with her fingers. I was watching her carefully, and when she hit what I guessed was the appendix place, I let out a yelp that rattled the window-panes. 'Ow! Ow! Ow!' I cried out. 'Don't, Matron, don't!' Then I slipped in the clincher. 'I've been sick all morning,' I moaned, 'and now there's nothing left to be sick with, but I still feel sick!'

This was the right move. I saw her hesitate. 'Stay where you are,' she said and she walked quickly from the room. She may have been a foul and beastly woman, but she had had a nurse's training and she didn't want a ruptured appendix on her hands.

Within an hour, the doctor arrived and he went through the same prodding and poking and I did my yelping at what I thought were the proper times. Then he put a thermometer in my mouth.

'Hmm,' he said. 'It reads normal. Let me feel your stomach once more.'

'Owch!' I screamed when he touched the vital spot.

The doctor went away with the Matron. The Matron returned half an hour later and said, 'The Headmaster has telephoned your mother and she's coming to fetch you this afternoon.'

I didn't answer her. I just lay there trying to look very ill, but my heart was singing out with all sorts of wonderful songs of praise and joy.

I was taken home across the Bristol Channel on the paddle-steamer and I felt so wonderful at being away from that dreaded school building that I very nearly forgot I was meant to be ill. That afternoon I had a session with Dr Dunbar at his surgery in Cathedral Road, Cardiff, and I tried the same tricks all over again. But Dr Dunbar was far wiser and more skilful than either the Matron or the school doctor. After he had prodded my stomach and I had done my yelping routine, he said to me, 'Now you can get dressed again and seat yourself on that chair.'

He himself sat down behind his desk and fixed me with a penetrating but not unkindly eye. 'You're faking, aren't you?' he said.

'How do you know?' I blurted out.

'Because your stomach is soft and perfectly normal,' he answered. 'If you had had an inflammation down there, the stomach would have been hard and rigid. It's quite easy to tell.'

I kept silent.

'I expect you're homesick,' he said.

I nodded miserably.

'Everyone is at first,' he said. 'You have to stick it out. And don't blame your mother for sending you away to boarding-school. She insisted you were too young to go, but it was I who persuaded her it was the right thing to do. Life is tough, and the sooner you learn how to cope with it the better for you.'

'What will you tell the school?' I asked him, trembling.

'I'll say you had a very severe infection of the stomach which I am curing with pills,' he answered smiling. 'It will mean that you must stay home for three more days. But promise me you won't try anything like this again. Your mother has enough on her hands without having to rush over to fetch you out of school.'

'I promise,' I said. 'I'll never do it again.'

I'm taking the Calsium, but have'nt needed one of the pills yet.

PILLS

A drive in the motor-car

Somehow or other I got through the first term at St Peter's, and towards the end of December my mother came over on the paddle-boat to take me and my trunk home for the Christmas holidays.

Dear Mama   Dec 9th

Just to make it a bit planer, I will be coming home on Dec 17th not the 18th. I will drive a Cardiff a four O'clock please meet me, if that is not quite planer safe nouse let me know what you want to know about it.

Love from Boy

Oh the bliss and the wonder of being with the family once again after all those weeks of fierce discipline! Unless you have been to boarding-school when you are very young, it is absolutely impossible to appreciate the delights of living

at home. It is almost *worth* going away because it's so lovely coming back. I could hardly believe that I didn't have to wash in cold water in the mornings or keep silent in the corridors, or say 'Sir' to every grown-up man I met, or use a chamber-pot in the bedroom, or get flicked with wet towels while naked in the changing-room, or eat porridge for breakfast that seemed to be full of little round lumpy grey sheep's-droppings, or walk all day long in perpetual fear of the long yellow cane that lay on top of the corner-cupboard in the Headmaster's study.

The weather was exceptionally mild that Christmas holiday and one amazing morning our whole family got ready to go for our first drive in the first motor-car we had ever owned. This

In *Danny the Champion of the World*, Danny was even younger than Roald Dahl's sister when he took to the road.

'I will not pretend I wasn't petrified. I was. But mixed in with the awful fear was a glorious feeling of excitement. Most of the really exciting things we do in our lives scare us to death. They wouldn't be exciting if they didn't. I sat very stiff and upright in my seat, gripping the steering-wheel tight with both hands. My eyes were about level with the top of the steering-wheel. I could have done with a cushion to raise me up higher, but it was too late for that.'

new motor-car was an enormous long black French automobile called a De Dion-Bouton which had a canvas roof that folded back. The driver was to be that twelve-years-older-than-me half-sister (now aged twenty-one) who had recently had her appendix removed.

She had received two full half-hour lessons in driving from the man who delivered the car, and in that enlightened year of 1925 this was considered quite sufficient. Nobody had to take a driving-test. You were your own judge of competence, and as soon as you felt you were ready to go, off you jolly well went.

As we all climbed into the car, our excitement was so intense we could hardly bear it.

'How fast will it go?' we cried out. 'Will it do fifty miles an hour?'

'It'll do sixty!' the ancient sister answered. Her tone was so confident and cocky it should have scared us to death, but it didn't.

'Oh, let's make it do sixty!' we shouted. 'Will you promise to take us up to sixty?'

'We shall probably go faster than that,' the sister announced, pulling on her driving-gloves and tying a scarf over her head in the approved driving-fashion of the period.

The canvas hood had been folded back because of the mild weather, converting the car into a magnificent open tourer. Up front, there were three bodies in all, the driver behind the wheel, my half-brother (aged eighteen) and one of my sisters (aged twelve). In the back seat there were four more of us, my mother (aged forty), two small sisters (aged eight and five) and myself (aged nine). Our machine possessed one very special feature which I don't think you see on the cars of today. This was a second windscreen in the back solely to keep the breeze off the faces of the back-seat passengers when the hood was down. It had a long centre section and two little end sections that could be angled backwards to deflect the wind.

Roald Dahl's favourite car as a grown-up was a BMW.

Drivers and cars had to be licensed in Britain from 1903 – but nobody was actually **tested** to see if they could drive a car until 1934.

We were all quivering with fear and joy as the driver let out the clutch and the great long black automobile leaned forward and stole into motion.

'Are you sure you know how to do it?' we shouted. 'Do you know where the brakes are?'

'Be quiet!' snapped the ancient sister. 'I've got to concentrate!'

Down the drive we went and out into the village of Llandaff itself. Fortunately there were very few vehicles on the roads in those days. Occasionally you met a small truck or a delivery-van and now and again a private car, but the danger of colliding with anything else was fairly remote so long as you kept the car on the road.

The splendid black tourer crept slowly through the village with the driver pressing the rubber bulb of the horn every time we passed a human being, whether it was the butcher-boy on his bicycle or just a pedestrian strolling on the pavement. Soon we were entering a countryside of green fields and high hedges with not a soul in sight.

'You didn't think I could do it, did you?' cried the ancient sister, turning round and grinning at us all.

'Now you keep your eyes on the road,' my mother said nervously.

'Go faster!' we shouted. 'Go on! Make her go faster! Put your foot down! We're only doing *fifteen miles an hour!*'

Spurred on by our shouts and taunts, the ancient sister began to increase the speed. The engine roared and the body vibrated. The driver was clutching the steering-wheel as though it were the hair of a drowning man, and we all watched the speedometer needle creeping up to twenty, then twenty-five, then thirty. We were probably doing about thirty-five miles an hour when we came suddenly to a sharpish bend in

Roald Dahl bought a car in 1936 – for the grand sum of £14. He must have been one of the very first people to take the new driving test.

the road. The ancient sister, never having been faced with a situation like this before, shouted 'Help!' and slammed on the brakes and swung the wheel wildly round. The rear wheels locked and went into a fierce sideways skid, and then, with a marvellous crunch of mudguards and metal, we went crashing into the hedge. The front passengers all shot through the front windscreen and the back passengers all shot through the back windscreen. Glass (there was

no Triplex then) flew in all directions and so did we. My brother and one sister landed on the bonnet of the car, someone else was catapulted out on to the road and at least one small sister landed in the middle of the hawthorn hedge. But miraculously nobody was hurt very much except me. My nose had been cut almost clean off my face as I went through the rear windscreen and now it was hanging on only by a single small thread of skin. My mother disentangled herself from the scrimmage and grabbed a handkerchief from her purse. She clapped the dangling nose back into place fast and held it there.

Not a cottage or a person was in sight, let alone a telephone. Some kind of bird started twittering in a tree farther down the road, otherwise all was silent.

My mother was bending over me in the rear seat and saying, 'Lean back and keep your head still.' To the ancient sister she said, 'Can you get this thing going again?'

The sister pressed the starter and to everyone's surprise, the engine fired.

'Back it out of the hedge,' my mother said. 'And hurry.'

The sister had trouble finding reverse gear. The cogs were grinding against one another with a fearful noise of tearing metal.

The Dahl family moved away from Cumberland Lodge in Llandaff in 1927. They stayed for a few weeks at '17, The Park', in Golders Green, north-west London, while Mrs Dahl was finding a house that would be right for her large family. She settled on this one – a house called 'Oakwood' in Heath Road, Bexley. Now the journey to school in Derbyshire was over 100 miles from home!

'I've never actually driven it backwards,' she admitted at last.

Everyone with the exception of the driver, my mother and me was out of the car and standing on the road. The noise of gear-wheels grinding against each other was terrible. It sounded as though a lawn-mower was being driven over hard rocks. The ancient sister was using bad words and going crimson in the face, but then my brother leaned his head over the driver's door and said, 'Don't you have to put your foot on the clutch?'

The harassed driver depressed the clutch-pedal and the gears meshed and one second later the great black beast leapt backwards out of the hedge and careered across the road into the hedge on the other side.

'Try to keep cool,' my mother said. 'Go forward slowly.'

At last the shattered motor-car was driven out of the second hedge and stood sideways across the road, blocking the highway. A man with a horse and cart now appeared on the scene and the man dismounted from his cart and walked across to our car and leaned over the rear door. He had a big drooping moustache and he wore a small black bowler-hat.

'You're in a fair old mess 'ere, ain't you?' he said to my mother.

'Can you drive a motor-car?' my mother asked him.

'Nope,' he said. 'And you're blockin' up the 'ole road. I've got a thousand fresh-laid heggs in this cart and I want to get 'em to market before noon.'

'Get out of the way,' my mother told him. 'Can't you see there's a child in here who's badly injured?'

'One thousand fresh-laid heggs,' the man repeated, staring straight at my mother's hand and the blood-soaked handkerchief and the blood running down her wrist. 'And if I don't get 'em to market by noon today I won't be able to sell 'em till next week. Then they won't be fresh-laid any more, will they? I'll be stuck with one thousand stale ole heggs that nobody wants.'

'I hope they all go rotten,' my mother said. 'Now back that cart out of our way this instant!' And to the children standing on the road she cried out, 'Jump back into the car! We're going to the doctor!'

'There's glass all over the seats!' they shouted.

'Never mind the glass!' my mother said. 'We've got to get this boy to the doctor fast!'

The passengers crawled back into the car. The man with the horse and cart backed off to a safe distance. The ancient sister managed to straighten the vehicle and get it pointed in the right direction, and then at last the once magnificent automobile tottered down the highway and headed for Dr Dunbar's surgery in Cathedral Road, Cardiff.

'I've never driven in a city,' the ancient and trembling sister announced.

'You are about to do so,' my mother said. 'Keep going.'

Proceeding at no more than four miles an hour all the way, we finally made it to Dr Dunbar's house. I was hustled out of the car and in through the front door with my mother still holding the bloodstained handkerchief firmly over my wobbling nose.

'Good heavens!' cried Dr Dunbar. 'It's been cut clean off!'

'It hurts,' I moaned.

'He can't go round without a nose for the rest of his life!' the doctor said to my mother.

'It looks as though he may have to,' my mother said.

'Nonsense!' the doctor told her. 'I shall sew it on again.'

'Can you do that?' my mother asked him.

'I can try,' he answered. 'I shall tape it on tight for now and

Roald Dahl's nose took a lot of stick. After nearly being chopped off in the car accident, it was bashed in when his **plane crash-landed** during the **Second World War**. After the crash, the **surgeon** rebuilt his nose in the style of silent-film star **Rudolf Valentino**.

Source: BFI Stills

I'll be up at your house with my assistant within the hour.'

Huge strips of sticking-plaster were strapped across my face to hold the nose in position. Then I was led back into the car and we crawled the two miles home to Llandaff.

About an hour later I found myself lying upon that same nursery table my ancient sister had occupied some months before for her appendix operation. Strong hands held me down while a mask stuffed with cotton-wool was clamped over my face. I saw a hand above me holding a bottle with white liquid in it and the liquid was being poured on to the cotton-wool inside the mask. Once again I smelled the sickly stench of chloroform and ether, and a voice was saying, 'Breathe deeply. Take some nice deep breaths.'

Chloroform is also known as trichloromethane and methyl trichloride. Scientists call the mixture of chemicals $CHCl3$. It was once widely used as an anaesthetic.

I fought fiercely to get off that table but my shoulders were pinned down by the full weight of a large man. The hand that was holding the bottle above my face kept tilting it farther and farther forward and the white liquid dripped and dripped on to the cotton-wool. Blood-red circles began to appear before my eyes and the circles started to spin round and round until they made a scarlet whirlpool with a deep black hole in the centre, and miles away in the distance a voice was saying, 'That's a good boy. We're nearly there now . . . we're nearly there . . . just close your eyes and go to sleep . . . '

I woke up in my own bed with my anxious mother sitting beside me, holding my hand. 'I didn't think you were ever going to come round,' she said. 'You've been asleep for more than eight hours.'

'Did Dr Dunbar sew my nose on again?' I asked her.

'Yes,' she said.

'Will it stay on?'

'He says it will. How do you feel, my darling?'

'Sick,' I said.

After I had vomited into a small basin, I felt a little better.

'Look under your pillow,' my mother said, smiling.

I turned and lifted a corner of my pillow, and underneath it, on the snow-white sheet, there lay a beautiful golden sovereign with the head of King George V on its uppermost side.

A 1925 **gold sovereign** could now be worth as much as £300.

'That's for being brave,' my mother said. 'You did very well. I'm proud of you.'

The Meccano Chariot

As I write, I am remembering something I did during
the Christmas holidays when I was either nine or ten,
I can't be sure which. For Christmas that year I had
been given a fine Meccano set as my main present, and
I lay in bed that night after the celebrations were over
thinking that I must build something with my new Meccano
that had never been built before. In the end I decided
I would make a device that was capable of 'bombing' from
the air the pedestrians using the public footpath across
our land.

   Briefly my plan was as follows: I would stretch a wire
all the way from the high roof of our house to the old
garage on the other side of the footpath. Then I would
construct from my Meccano a machine that would hang from
the wire by a grooved wheel (there was such a wheel in my
Meccano box) and this machine would hopefully run down
the wire at great speed dropping its bombs on the unwary
walkers underneath.

   Next morning, filled with the enthusiasm that grips all
great inventors, I climbed on to the roof of our house
by the skylight and wrapped one end of the long roll of
wire around a chimney. I threw the rest of the wire into
the garden below and went back down myself through the
skylight. I carried the wire across the garden, over the
fence, across the footpath, over the next fence and into
our land on the other side. I now pulled the wire very
tight and fixed it with a big nail to the top of the door

of the old garage. The total length of the wire was about one hundred yards. So far so good.

Next I set about constructing from the Meccano my bombing machine, or chariot as I called it. I put the wheel at the top, and then running down from the wheel I made a strong column about two feet long. At the lower end of this column, I fixed two arms that projected outwards at right angles, one on either side, and along these arms I suspended five empty Heinz soup tins. The whole thing looked something like this:

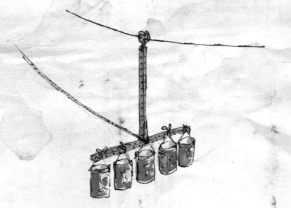

I carried it up to the roof and hung it on the wire. Then I attached one end of a ball of string to the lower end of the chariot and let it rip, playing out the string as it went. It was wonderful. Because the wire sloped steeply from the roof of the house all the way to the other end, the chariot careered down the wire at terrific speed, across the garden and over the footpath, and it didn't stop until it hit the old garage door on the far side. Great. I was ready to go.

With the string, I hauled the chariot back to the roof. And now, from a jug I filled all the five soup tins with

water. I lay flat on the roof waiting for a victim. I knew
I wouldn't have to wait long because the footpath was much
used by people taking their dogs for walks in the wood
beyond.

Soon two ladies dressed in tweed skirts and jackets
and each wearing a hat, came strolling up the path with
a revolting little Pekinese dog on a lead. I knew I had
to time this carefully, so when they were very nearly but
not quite directly under the wire, I let my chariot go.
Down she went, making a wonderful screeching-humming noise
as the metal wheel ran down the wire and the string ran
through my fingers at great speed. Bombing from a height is
never easy. I had to guess when my chariot was directly
over the target, and when that moment came, I jerked the
string. The chariot stopped dead and the tins swung upside
down and all the water tipped out. The ladies, who had
halted and looked up on hearing the rushing noise of my
chariot overhead, caught the cascade of water full in
their faces. It was tremendous. A bull's-eye first time.
The women screamed. I lay flat on the roof so as not to be
seen, peering over the edge, and I saw the women shouting
and waving their arms. Then they came marching straight
into our garden through the gate at the back and crossed
the garden and hammered on the door. I nipped down smartly
through the skylight and did a bunk.

Later on, at lunch, my mother fixed me with a steely
eye and told me she was confiscating my Meccano set for
the rest of the holidays. But for days afterwards I
experienced the pleasant warm glow that comes to all of us
when we have brought off a major triumph.

Captain Hardcastle

We called them masters in those days, not teachers, and at St Peter's the one I feared most of all, apart from the Headmaster, was Captain Hardcastle.

This man was slim and wiry and he played football. On the football field he wore white running shorts and white gymshoes and short white socks. His legs were as hard and thin as ram's legs and the skin around his calves was almost exactly the colour of mutton fat. The hair on his head was not ginger. It was a brilliant dark vermilion, like a ripe orange, and it was plastered back with immense quantities of brilliantine in the same fashion as the Headmaster's. The parting in his hair was a white line straight down the middle of the scalp, so straight it could only have been made with a ruler. On either side of the parting you could see the comb tracks running back through the greasy orange hair like little tramlines.

Captain Hardcastle sported a moustache that was the

Brilliantine is an old-fashioned hair gel favoured by gentlemen when Roald Dahl was a boy. It is very oily and and makes hair look very greasy.

123

Captain Hardcastle's real name was Lancaster. Roald Dahl changed it in *Boy*, perhaps because he describes him in such terrifying detail. He created a similarly foul teacher – called 'Captain Lancaster' – in *Danny the Champion of the World*:

'*He had fiery carrot-coloured hair and a little clipped carrotty moustache and a fiery temper . . . Captain Lancaster was a violent man, and we were all terrified of him. He used to sit at his desk stroking his carrotty moustache and watching us with pale watery-blue eyes, searching for trouble. And as he sat there, he would make queer snuffling grunts through his nose, like some dog sniffing round a rabbit hole.*'

same colour as his hair, and oh what a moustache it was! A truly terrifying sight, a thick orange hedge that sprouted and flourished between his nose and his upper lip and ran clear across his face from the middle of one cheek to the middle of the other. But this was not one of those nailbrush moustaches, all short and clipped and bristly. Nor was it long and droopy in the walrus style. Instead, it was curled most splendidly upwards all the way along as though it had had a permanent wave put into it or possibly curling tongs heated in the mornings over a tiny flame of methylated spirits. The only other way he could have achieved this curling effect, we boys decided, was by prolonged upward brushing with a hard toothbrush in front of the looking-glass every morning.

Behind the moustache there lived an inflamed and savage face with a deeply corrugated brow that indicated a very limited intelligence. 'Life is a puzzlement,' the corrugated brow seemed to be saying, 'and the world is a dangerous place. All men are enemies and small boys are insects that will turn and bite you if you don't get them first and squash them hard.'

Captain Hardcastle was never still. His orange head twitched and jerked perpetually from side to side in the most alarming fashion, and each twitch was accompanied by a little grunt that came out of the nostrils. He had been a soldier in the army in the Great War and that, of course, was how he had received his title. But even small insects like us knew that 'Captain' was not a very exalted rank and only a man with little else to boast about would hang on to it in civilian life. It was bad enough to keep calling yourself 'Major' after it was all over, but 'Captain' was the bottoms.

Rumour had it that the constant twitching and jerking and snorting was caused by something called shell-shock, but we were not quite sure what that was. We took it to mean that an explosive object had gone off very close to him with such an enormous bang that it had made him jump high in the air and he hadn't stopped jumping since.

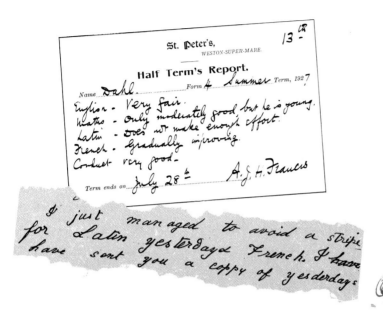

St. Peter's, WESTON-SUPER-MARE.

13

Half Term's Report.

Name *Dahl.* Form *4* *Summer* Term, 192*7*

English - *Very fair.*
Maths - *Only moderately good but he is young.*
Latin - *Does not make enough effort.*
French - *Gradually improving.*
Conduct - *very good -*

Term ends on *July 28th* *A.S.H. Francis*

I just managed to avoid a stripe for Latin yesterday. French. I have sent you a copy of yesterday's

For a reason that I could never properly understand, Captain Hardcastle had it in for me from my very first day at St Peter's. Perhaps it was because he taught Latin and I was no good at it. Perhaps it was because already, at the age of nine, I was very nearly as tall as he was. Or even more likely, it was because I took an instant dislike to his giant orange moustache and he often caught me staring at it with what was probably a little sneer under the nose. I had only to pass within ten feet of him in the corridor and he would glare at me and shout, 'Hold yourself straight, boy! Pull your shoulders back!' or 'Take those hands out of your pockets!' or 'What's so funny, may I ask? What are you smirking at?' or most insulting of all, '*You,* what's-your-name, get on with your work!' I knew, therefore, that it was only a matter of time before the gallant Captain nailed me good and proper.

The crunch came during my second term when I was exactly nine and a half, and it happened during evening Prep. Every weekday evening, the whole school would sit for one hour in the Main Hall, between six and seven o'clock, to do Prep. The master on duty for the week would be in charge of Prep, which meant that he sat high up on a dais at the top end of the Hall and kept order. Some masters read a book while taking Prep and some corrected exercises, but not Captain Hardcastle. He would sit up there on the dais twitching and grunting and never once would he look down at his desk. His small milky-blue eyes would rove the Hall for the full sixty minutes, searching for trouble, and heaven help the boy who caused it.

The rules of Prep were simple but strict. You were forbidden to look up from your work, and you were forbidden to talk. That was all there was to it, but it left you precious little leeway. In extreme circumstances, and I never knew what these were, you could put your hand up and wait until you were asked to speak but you had better be awfully sure that the circumstances were extreme. Only twice during my four years at St Peter's did I see a boy putting up his hand during Prep. The first one went like this:

MASTER. What is it?
BOY. Please sir, may I be excused to go to the lavatory?
MASTER. Certainly not. You should have gone before.
BOY. But sir . . . please sir . . .I didn't want to before . . . I didn't know . . .
MASTER. Whose fault was that? Get on with your work!
BOY. But sir . . .Oh sir . . . Please sir, let me go!

If **homework** is done at home, then what is the name for homework that is done at school . . . ? The answer is **prep**!

MASTER. One more word out of you and you'll be in trouble.

Naturally, the wretched boy dirtied his pants, which caused a storm later on upstairs with the Matron.

On the second occasion, I remember clearly that it was a summer term and the boy who put his hand up was called Braithwaite. I also seem to recollect that the master taking Prep was our friend Captain Hardcastle, but I wouldn't swear to it. The dialogue went something like this:

MASTER. Yes, what is it?

BRAITHWAITE. Please sir, a wasp came in through the window and it's stung me on my lip and it's swelling up.

MASTER. A *what*?

BRAITHWAITE. A wasp, sir.

MASTER. Speak up, boy, I can't hear you! A *what* came in through the window?

BRAITHWAITE. It's hard to speak up, sir, with my lip all swelling up.

MASTER. With your *what* all swelling up? Are you trying to be funny?

BRAITHWAITE. No sir, I promise I'm not, sir.

MASTER. Talk properly, boy! What's the matter with you?

BRAITHWAITE. I've told you, sir. I've been stung, sir. My lip is swelling. It's hurting terribly.

MASTER. *Hurting terribly?* What's hurting terribly?

BRAITHWAITE. My lip, sir. It's getting bigger and bigger.

MASTER. What Prep are you doing tonight?

BRAITHWAITE. French verbs, sir. We have to write them out.

MASTER. Do you write with your lip?

BRAITHWAITE. No sir, I don't sir, but you see . . .

MASTER. All I see is that you are making an infernal noise and disturbing everybody in the room. Now get on with your work.

They were tough, those masters, make no mistake about it, and if you wanted to survive, you had to become pretty tough yourself.

My own turn came, as I said, during my second term and Captain Hardcastle was again taking Prep. You should know that during Prep every boy in the Hall sat at his own small individual wooden desk. These desks had the usual sloping wooden tops with a narrow flat strip at the far end where there was a groove to hold your pen and a small hole in the right-hand side in which the ink-well sat. The pens we used had detachable nibs and it was necessary to dip your nib into the ink-well every six or seven seconds when you were writing. Ball-point pens and felt pens had not then been invented, and fountain-pens were forbidden. The nibs we used were very fragile and most boys kept a supply of new ones in a small box in their trouser pockets.

Prep was in progress. Captain Hardcastle was sitting up on the dais in front of us, stroking his orange moustache, twitching his head and grunting through his nose. His eyes roved the Hall endlessly, searching for mischief. The only noises to be heard were Captain Hardcastle's little snorting grunts and the soft sound of pen-nibs moving over paper. Occasionally there was a *ping* as somebody dipped his nib too violently into his tiny white porcelain ink-well.

Disaster struck when I foolishly stubbed the tip of my nib

Ball-point pens were first developed in 1888. But it wasn't until 1938, when László Biró – a Hungarian newspaper editor – came up with a better model, which stopped ink going everywhere.

into the top of the desk. The nib broke. I knew I hadn't got a spare one in my pocket, but a broken nib was never accepted as an excuse for not finishing Prep. We had been set an essay to write and the subject was 'The Life Story of a Penny' (I still have that essay in my files). I had made a decent start and I was rattling along fine when I broke that nib. There was still another half-hour of Prep to go and I couldn't sit there doing nothing all that time. Nor could I put up my hand and tell Captain Hardcastle I had broken my nib. I simply did not dare. And as a matter of fact, I really *wanted* to finish that essay. I knew exactly what was going to happen to my penny through the next two pages and I couldn't bear to leave it unsaid.

Turn over the page to read 'The Life Story of a Penny'!

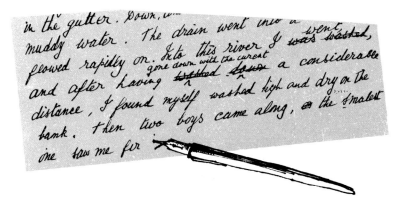

I glanced to my right. The boy next to me was called Dobson. He was the same age as me, nine and a half, and a nice fellow. Even now, sixty years later, I can still remember that Dobson's father was a doctor and that he lived, as I had learnt from the label on Dobson's tuck-box, at The Red House, Uxbridge, Middlesex.

Dobson's desk was almost touching mine. I thought I would risk it. I kept my head lowered but watched Captain Hardcastle very carefully. When I was fairly sure he was looking the other way, I put a hand in front of my mouth and whispered, 'Dobson

Here is 'The Life Story of a Penny' from Roald Dahl's essay book.
(He wrote it in 1926, aged nine and a half.)

The Life Story of a Penny

One hot day in the month of July, when the men of our copper mine in South America were digging into the depths thereof, I felt something hard strike me underneath. I was shovelled up into a truck, being only a small lump of copper, and was conveyed to Rio de Janeiro where I was shipped to England amongst a heap of copper.

The ship having arrived at Liverpool, I was taken to 'the mint' in London, and in a merciful manner I was cast into a roaring furnace. I was left there till quite white hot, when finally I began to melt.

I was taken out and had a picture of King George V's head stamped cruelly on one side of me and Britannia on the other.

I was then sent to be put in a drawer in the Midland Bank, looking very shiny, but soon got that brown colour that pennies get, when mixed up with a great many other coins. A large and fat lady came into the bank one afternoon, and handed the man a cheque for a penny.

I was handed to the lady who dropped me carefully into her purse. Having remained in the purse for a certain time, I was taken out, greatly to my astonishment I found myself in a fishmonger's shop, the lady had used me to pay for some shrimps she had bought.

Next time I was taken out of the fishmonger's drawer, I was handed to a little boy, probably for change. I was placed in his pocket with a rusty old knife, a piece of string and a shilling. This boy being stupid, was rolling me along the street when suddenly I disappeared from the boy's sight, I had fallen down a drain into the gutter. Down, and down I went amidst the muddy water. The drain went into a river, which flowed rapidly on. Into this river I went and after having gone down with the current a considerable distance, I found myself washed high and dry on the bank. Then two boys came along, the smallest one saw me fir

What happened next? We'll never know what became of Roald Dahl's penny because his nib broke . . .

. . . Dobson . . . Could you lend me a nib?'

Suddenly there was an explosion up on the dais. Captain Hardcastle had leapt to his feet and was pointing at me and shouting, 'You're talking! I saw you talking! Don't try to deny it! I distinctly saw you talking behind your hand!'

I sat there frozen with terror.

Every boy stopped working and looked up.

Captain Hardcastle's face had gone from red to deep purple and he was twitching violently.

'Do you deny you were talking?' he shouted.

'No, sir, no, b-but . . .'

'And do you deny you were trying to cheat? Do you deny you were asking Dobson for help with your work?'

'N-no, sir, I wasn't. I wasn't cheating.'

'Of course you were cheating! Why else, may I ask, would you be speaking to Dobson? I take it you were not inquiring after his health?'

It is worth reminding the reader once again of my age. I was not a self-possessed lad of fourteen. Nor was I twelve or even ten years old. I was nine and a half, and at that age one is ill equipped to tackle a grown-up man with flaming orange hair and a violent temper. One can do little else but stutter.

'I . . . I have broken my nib, sir,' I whispered. 'I . . . I was asking Dobson if he c-could lend me one, sir.'

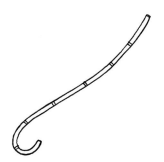

'You are lying!' cried Captain Hardcastle, and there was triumph in his voice. 'I always knew you were a liar! *And* a cheat as well!'

'All I w-wanted was a nib, sir.'

'I'd shut up if I were you!' thundered the voice on the dais. 'You'll only get yourself into deeper trouble! I am giving you a Stripe!'

These were words of doom. A Stripe! *I am giving you a*

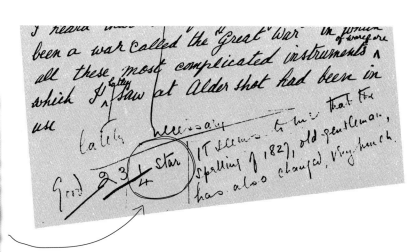

Stripe! All around, I could feel a kind of sympathy reaching out to me from every boy in the school, but nobody moved or made a sound.

Here I must explain the system of Stars and Stripes that we had at St Peter's. For exceptionally good work, you could be awarded a Quarter-Star, and a red dot was made with crayon beside your name on the notice-board. If you got four Quarter-Stars, a red line was drawn through the four dots indicating that you had completed your Star.

Roald Dahl won a prize in 1927 for earning fourteen Quarter-Stars in one term.

After Roald Dahl's essay on 'A person who has lived in 1827 suddenly entering life now', **Mr Corrado** wrote, '*It seems to me that the spelling of 1827, old gentleman, has also changed, very much.*'

For exceptionally poor work or bad behaviour, you were given a Stripe, and that automatically meant a thrashing from the Headmaster.

Every master had a book of Quarter-Stars and a book of Stripes, and these had to be filled in and signed and torn out exactly like cheques from a cheque book. The Quarter-Stars were pink, the Stripes were a fiendish, blue-green colour. The boy who received a Star or a Stripe would pocket it until the following morning after prayers, when the Headmaster would call upon anyone who had been given one or the other to come forward in front of the whole school and hand it in. Stripes were considered so dreadful that they were not given very often. In any one week it was unusual for more than two or three boys to receive Stripes.

And now Captain Hardcastle was giving one to me.

'Come here,' he ordered.

I got up from my desk and walked to the dais. He already had his book of Stripes on the desk and was filling one out. He was using red ink, and along the line where it said *Reason*, he wrote, *Talking in Prep, trying to cheat and lying.* He signed it and tore it out of the book. Then, taking plenty of time, he filled in the counterfoil. He picked up the terrible piece of green-blue paper and waved it in my direction but he didn't look up. I

The records show that Roald Dahl was awarded a **Stripe** by Captain Lancaster in June 1926 for '3 warnings in a week'.

took it out of his hand and walked back to my desk. The eyes of the whole school followed my progress.

For the remainder of Prep I sat at my desk and did nothing. Having no nib, I was unable to write another word about 'The Life Story of a Penny', but I was made to finish it the next afternoon instead of playing games.

The following morning, as soon as prayers were over, the Headmaster called for Quarter-Stars and Stripes. I was the only boy to go up. The assistant masters were sitting on very upright chairs on either side of the Headmaster, and I caught a glimpse of Captain Hardcastle, arms folded across his chest, head twitching, the milky-blue eyes watching me intently, the look of triumph still glimmering on his face. I handed in my Stripe. The Headmaster took it and read the writing. 'Come and see me in my study,' he said, 'as soon as this is over.'

Five minutes later, walking on my toes and trembling terribly, I passed through the green baize door and entered the sacred precincts where the Headmaster lived. I knocked on his study door.

'Enter!'

I turned the knob and went into this large square room with bookshelves and easy chairs and the gigantic desk topped in red leather straddling the far corner. The Headmaster was sitting behind the desk holding my Stripe in his fingers. 'What have you got to say for yourself?' he asked me, and the white shark's teeth flashed dangerously between his lips.

'I didn't lie, sir,' I said. 'I promise I didn't. And I wasn't trying to cheat.'

'Captain Hardcastle says you were doing both,' the Headmaster said. 'Are you calling Captain Hardcastle a liar?'

'No, sir. Oh no, sir.'

'I wouldn't if I were you.'

The cane wasn't the only instrument of torture in schools. Other options were the slipper, the strap (a wide, heavy strip of leather) and the birch (a bundle of leafless twigs). The tawse was a truly wicked device – a strip of leather with one end sliced into many smaller strips. They are all now banned.

The slipper worked best if there was no foot in it at the time of thwacking.

'I had broken my nib, sir, and I was asking Dobson if he could lend me another.'

'That is not what Captain Hardcastle says. He says you were asking for help with your essay.'

'Oh no, sir, I wasn't. I was a long way away from Captain Hardcastle and I was only whispering. I don't think he could have heard what I said, sir.'

'So you *are* calling him a liar.'

'Oh no, sir! No, sir! I would never do that!'

It was impossible for me to win against the Headmaster. What I would like to have said was, 'Yes, sir, if you really want to know, sir, I *am* calling Captain Hardcastle a liar because that's what he is!', but it was out of the question. I did, however, have one trump card left to play, or I thought I did.

'You could ask Dobson, sir,' I whispered.

'*Ask Dobson?*' he cried. 'Why should I ask Dobson?'

'He would tell you what I said, sir.'

'Captain Hardcastle is an officer and a gentleman,' the Headmaster said. 'He has told me what happened. I hardly think I want to go round asking some silly little boy if Captain Hardcastle is speaking the truth.'

I kept silent.

'For talking in Prep,' the Headmaster went on, 'for trying to cheat and for lying, I am going to give you six strokes of the cane.'

He rose from his desk and crossed over to the corner-cupboard on the opposite side of the study. He reached up and took from the top of it three very thin yellow canes, each with the bent-over handle at one end. For a few seconds, he held them in his hands, examining them with some care, then he selected one and replaced the other two on top of the cupboard.

'Six of the best' was one of the worst punishments ever. After such a serious caning, the recipient would have great difficulty sitting down.

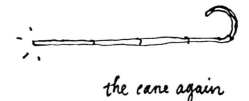

the cane again

'Bend over.'

I was frightened of that cane. There is no small boy in the world who wouldn't be. It wasn't simply an instrument for beating you. It was a weapon for wounding. It lacerated the skin. It caused severe black and scarlet bruising that took three weeks to disappear, and all the time during those three weeks, you could feel your heart beating along the wounds.

I tried once more, my voice slightly hysterical now. 'I didn't do it, sir! I swear I'm telling the truth!'

'Be quiet and bend over! Over there! And touch your toes!'

Very slowly, I bent over. Then I shut my eyes and braced myself for the first stroke.

Crack! It was like a rifle shot! With a very hard stroke of the cane on one's buttocks, the time-lag before you feel any pain is about four seconds. Thus, the experienced caner will always pause between strokes to allow the agony to reach its peak.

So for a few seconds after the first *crack* I felt virtually nothing. Then suddenly came the frightful searing agonizing unbearable burning across the buttocks, and as it reached its highest and most excruciating point, the second *crack* came down. I clutched hold of my ankles as tight as I could and I bit into my lower lip. I was determined not to make a sound, for that would only give the executioner greater satisfaction.

Crack! . . . Five seconds pause.

A cane was usually made of **bamboo** or **rattan**. It was very bendy, to ensure maximum **sting**.

Crack! . . . Another pause.

Crack! . . . And another pause.

I was counting the strokes, and as the sixth one hit me, I knew I was going to survive in silence.

'That will do,' the voice behind me said.

I straightened up and clutched my backside as hard as I possibly could with both hands. This is always the instinctive and automatic reaction. The pain is so frightful you try to grab hold of it and tear it away, and the tighter you squeeze, the more it helps.

I did not look at the Headmaster as I hopped across the thick red carpet towards the door. The door was closed and nobody was about to open it for me, so for a couple of seconds I had to let go of my bottom with one hand to turn the door-knob. Then I was out and hopping around in the hallway of the private sanctum.

Directly across the hall from the Headmaster's study was the assistant masters' Common Room. They were all in there now waiting to spread out to their respective classrooms, but what I couldn't help noticing, even in my agony, was that *this door was open.*

Why was it open?

Had it been left that way on purpose so that they could all hear more clearly the sound of the cane from across the hall?

Of course it had. And I felt quite sure that it was Captain Hardcastle who had opened it. I pictured him standing in there among his colleagues snorting with satisfaction at every stinging stroke.

Small boys can be very comradely when a member of their community has got into trouble, and even more so when they feel an injustice has been done. When I returned to the classroom, I was surrounded on all sides by sympathetic faces

Corporal punishment (beating or hitting a child) as a form of discipline continued in British state schools until 1986. It was banned in all other schools in 1998, although by that time most schools had stopped using it anyway.

Douglas Highton was great friends with Roald Dahl at St Peter's. He was slightly older than Roald Dahl, but was in the same section. They went out on trips together, along with Highton's younger brother and mother. When Highton earned a scholarship to Oakham School, all the boys at St Peter's were given half a day's holiday to celebrate!

and voices, but one particular incident has always stayed with me. A boy of my own age called Highton was so violently incensed by the whole affair that he said to me before lunch that day, 'You don't have a father. I do. I am going to write to my father and tell him what has happened and he'll do something about it.'

'He couldn't do anything,' I said.

'Oh yes he could,' Highton said. 'And what's more he will. My father won't let them get away with this.'

'Where is he now?'

'He's in Greece,' Highton said. 'In Athens. But that won't make any difference.'

Then and there, little Highton sat down and wrote to the father he admired so much, but of course nothing came of it. It was nevertheless a touching and generous gesture from one small boy to another and I have never forgotten it.

This is Roald Dahl's class.

How I Became a Writer

I have still got all my school reports from those days more than fifty years ago, and I've gone through them one by one, trying to discover a hint of promise for a future fiction writer. The subject to look at was obviously English Composition. But all my prep-school reports under this heading were flat and non-committal, excepting one. The one that took my eye was dated Christmas Term, 1928. I was then twelve, and my English teacher was Mr Victor Corrado, I remember him vividly, a tall, handsome athlete with black wavy hair and a Roman nose (who one night later on eloped with the matron, Miss Davis, and we never saw either of them again). Anyway, it so happened that Mr Corrado took us in boxing as well as in English Compositon, and in this particular report it said under English, 'See his report on boxing. Precisely the same marks apply.' So we look under Boxing, and there it says, 'Too slow and ponderous. His punches are not well-timed and are easily seen coming.'

But just once a week at this school, every Saturday morning, every beautiful and blessed Saturday morning, all the shivering horrors would disappear and for two glorious hours I would experience something that came very close to ecstasy.

Unfortunately, this did not happen until one was ten years old. But no matter. Let me tell you what it was.

At exactly ten-thirty on Saturday mornings, Mr Pople's infernal bell would go *clangetty-clang-clang*. This was a signal for the following to take place:

First, all boys of nine and under (about seventy all

told) would proceed at once to the large outdoor asphalt playground behind the main building. Standing on the playground with legs apart and arms folded across her mountainous bosom was Miss Davis, the matron. If it was raining, the boys were expected to arrive in raincoats. If snowing or blowing a blizzard, then it was coats and scarves. And school caps, of course – grey with a red badge on the front – had always to be worn. But no Act of God, neither tornado nor hurricane nor volcanic eruption was ever allowed to stop those ghastly two-hour Saturday morning walks that the seven-, eight- and nine-year-old little boys had to take along the windy esplanades of Weston-super-Mare on Saturday mornings. They walked in crocodile formation, two by two, with Miss Davis striding alongside in tweed skirt and woollen stockings and a felt hat that must surely have been nibbled by rats.

The other thing that happened when Mr Pople's bell rang out on Saturday mornings was that the rest of the boys, all those of ten and over (about one hundred all told) would go immediately to the main Assembly Hall and sit down. A junior master called S. K. Jopp would then poke his head around the door and shout at us with such ferocity that specks of spit would fly from his mouth like bullets and splash against the window panes across the room. 'All right!' he shouted. 'No talking! No moving! Eyes front and hands on desks!' Then out he would pop again.

We sat still and waited. We were waiting for the lovely time we knew would be coming soon. Outside in the driveway we heard the motor-cars being started up. All were ancient. All had to be cranked by hand. (The year, don't forget, was around 1927/28.) This was a Saturday

morning ritual. There were five cars in all, and into
them would pile the entire staff of fourteen masters,
including not only the Headmaster himself but also the
purple-faced Mr Pople*. Then off they would roar in
a cloud of blue smoke and come to rest outside a pub
called, if I remember rightly, 'The Bewhiskered Earl'.
There they would remain until just before lunch, drinking
pint after pint of strong brown ale. And two and a half
hours later, at one o'clock, we would watch them coming
back, walking very carefully into the dining-room for
lunch, holding on to things as they went.

So much for the masters. But what of us, the great
mass of ten-, eleven- and twelve-year-olds left sitting
in the Assembly Hall in a school that was suddenly
without a single adult in the entire place? We knew, of
course, exactly what was going to happen next. Within a
minute of the departure of the masters, we would hear the
front door opening, and footsteps outside, and then, with
a flurry of loose clothes and jangling bracelets and flying
hair, a woman would burst into the room shouting, 'Hello,
everybody! Cheer up! This isn't a burial service!' or
words to that effect. And this was Mrs O'Connor.

Blessed beautiful Mrs O'Connor with her whacky
clothes and her grey hair flying in all directions.
She was about fifty years, with a horsey face and long
yellow teeth, but to us she was beautiful. She was not
on the staff. She was hired from somewhere in the
town to come up on Saturday mornings and be a sort of
baby-sitter, to keep us quiet for two and a half hours

*Mr Pople was a paunchy, crimson-faced individual who acted as a school-porter,
boiler superintendent and general handyman. His power stemmed from the fact that
he could (and he most certainly did) report us to the Headmaster upon the
slightest provocation.

while the masters went off boozing at the pub.

But Mrs O'Connor was no baby-sitter. She was nothing less than great and gifted teacher, a scholar and a lover of English Literature. Each of us with her every Saturday morning for three years) from the age of ten until we left the school) and during that time we spanned the entire history of English Literature from A.D. 597 to the early nineteenth century.

Newcomers to the class were given for keeps a slim blue book called simply *The Chronological Table*, and it contained only six pages. Those six pages were filled with a very long list in chronological order of all the great and not so great landmarks in English Literature, together with their dates. Exactly one hundred of these were chosen by Mrs O'Connor and we marked them in our books and learned them by heart. Here are a few that I still remember:

A.D. 597   St Augustine lands in Thanet and brings Christianity to Britain
  731   Bede's *Ecclesiastical History*
 1215   Signing of the *Magna Carta*
 1399   Langland's *Vision of Piers Plowman*
 1476   Caxton sets up first printing press at Westminster
 1478   Chaucer's *Canterbury Tales*
 1485   Malory's *Morte d'Arthur*
 1590   Spenser's *Faërie Queene*
 1623   First Folio of Shakespeare
 1667   Milton's *Paradise Lost*
 1668   Dryden's Essays
 1678   Bunyan's *Pilgrim's Progress*

```
1711  Addison's Spectator
1719  Defoe's Robinson Crusoe
1726  Swift's Gulliver's Travels
1733  Pope's Essay on Man
1755  Johnson's Dictionary
1791  Boswell's Life of Johnson
1833  Carlyle's Sartor Resartus
1859  Darwin's Origin of Species
```

Mrs O'Connor would then take each item in turn and spend one entire Saturday morning of two and a half hours talking to us about it. Thus, at the end of three years, with approximately thirty-six Saturdays in each school year, she would have covered the one hundred items.

And what marvellous exciting fun it was! She had the great teacher's knack of making everything she spoke about come alive to us in that room. In two and a half hours, we grew to love Langland and his Piers Plowman. The next Saturday, it was Chaucer, and we loved him, too. Even rather difficult fellows like Milton and Dryden and Pope all became thrilling when Mrs O'Connor told us about their lives and read parts of their work to us aloud. And the result of all this, for me at any rate, was that by the age of thirteen I had become intensely aware of the vast heritage of literature that had been built up in England over the centuries. I also became an avid and insatiable reader of good writing.

Dear lovely Mrs O'Connor! Perhaps it was worth going to that awful school simply to experience the joy of her Saturday mornings.

'Ellis and the Boil' was once part of a very early draft of *The Witches*, in which the hero is sent away to boarding school. But Roald Dahl decided to include the chapter in *Boy* instead.

Little Ellis and the boil

During my third term at St Peter's, I got flu and was put to bed in the Sick Room, where the dreaded Matron reigned supreme. In the next bed to mine was a seven-year-old boy called Ellis, whom I liked a lot. Ellis was there because he had an immense and angry-looking boil on the inside of his thigh. I saw it. It was as big as a plum and about the same colour.

One morning, in came the doctor to examine us, and sailing along beside him was the Matron. Her mountainous bosom was enclosed in a starched white envelope, and because of this she somehow reminded me of a painting I had once seen of a four-masted schooner in full canvas running before the wind.

'What's his temperature today?' the doctor asked, pointing at me.

'Just over a hundred, doctor,' the Matron told him.

'He's been up here long enough,' the doctor said. 'Send him back to school tomorrow.' Then he turned to Ellis. 'Take off your pyjama trousers,' he said. He was a very small doctor, with steel-rimmed spectacles and a bald head. He frightened the life out of me.

Ellis removed his pyjama trousers. The doctor bent forward and looked at the boil. 'Hmmm,' he said. 'That's a nasty one, isn't it? We're going to have to do something about that, aren't we, Ellis?'

'What are you going to do?' Ellis asked, trembling.

'Nothing for you to worry about,' the doctor said. 'Just lie back and take no notice of me.'

Little Ellis lay back with his head on the pillow. The doctor had put his bag on the floor at the end of Ellis's bed, and now he knelt down on the floor and opened the bag. Ellis, even when he lifted his head from the pillow, couldn't see what the doctor was doing there. He was hidden by the end of the bed. But I saw everything. I saw him take out a sort of scalpel which had a long steel handle and a small pointed blade. He crouched below the end of Ellis's bed, holding the scalpel in his right hand.

'Give me a large towel, Matron,' he said.

The Matron handed him a towel.

Still crouching low and hidden from little Ellis's view by the end of the bed, the doctor unfolded the towel and spread it over the palm of his left hand. In his right hand he held the scalpel.

Ellis was frightened and suspicious. He started raising himself up on his elbows to get a better look. 'Lie down, Ellis,' the doctor said, and even as he spoke, he bounced up from the end of the bed like a jack-in-the-box and flung the outspread towel straight into Ellis's face. Almost in the same second, he thrust his right arm forward and plunged the point of the scalpel deep into the centre of the enormous boil. He gave the blade a quick twist and then withdrew it again before the wretched boy had had time to disentangle his head from the towel.

Ellis screamed. He never saw the scalpel going in and he never saw it coming out, but he felt it all right and he screamed like a stuck pig. I can see him now struggling to get the towel off his head, and when he emerged the tears were streaming down his cheeks and his huge brown eyes were staring at the doctor with a look of utter and total outrage.

'Don't make such a fuss about nothing,' the Matron said.

'Put a dressing on it, Matron,' the doctor said, 'with plenty of mag sulph paste.' And he marched out of the room.

I couldn't really blame the doctor. I thought he handled things rather cleverly. Pain was something we were expected to endure. Anaesthetics and pain-killing injections were not much used in those days. Dentists, in particular, never

Magnesium sulphate paste draws out nasty impurities and poisons from the body. It can be used on boils – like with poor little Ellis – and carbuncles.

bothered with them. But I doubt very much if you would be entirely happy today if a doctor threw a towel in your face and jumped on you with a knife.

It must have been pretty grim being ill at boarding school. Roald Dahl often told his mother all about it in letters home.

The wart that Roald Dahl describes here was nothing compared to some of the other dreadful illnesses and operations that he and his family went through in later life.

a + he (wart) on my thum has come off beautifly, but the one on my knee has'nt even turned into a blister. You meant me to learn singing did'nt you.

Roald Dahl was particularly concerned about an outbreak of measles, a disease that children are now usually vaccinated against.

Feb. 25th 1928.

St. PETER'S.
WESTON-S-MARE.

Dear Mama,

Thanks for your letter. Most of the meazle boys are down, except about two, one Ragg² by name went up about a week ago, being the last boy who has'nt had it. Ford is still very bad, he got better on Friday but has again got very ill.

~~~~~ er Friday morning, and Hills horse cantered on it front,
~~~~~ up when he suddenly startes off at full
~~~~~ hieved at this and tried to catch
~~~~~ I hearly came
~~~~~ e, which

Goat's tobacco

When I was about nine, the ancient half-sister got engaged to be married. The man of her choice was a young English doctor and that summer he came with us to Norway.

This was Dr Arnold Ashley Miles, always known to the family as Ashley. He and Ellen married in 1930.

manly lover and ancient half-sister (in background)

Romance was floating in the air like moondust and the two lovers, for some reason we younger ones could never understand, did not seem to be very keen on us tagging along with them. They went out in the boat alone. They climbed the rocks alone. They even had breakfast alone. We resented this. As a family we had always done everything together and we didn't see why the ancient half-sister should suddenly decide to do things differently even if she had become engaged. We were inclined to blame the male lover for disrupting the calm of our family life, and it was inevitable that he would have to suffer for it sooner or later.

The male lover was a great pipe-smoker. The disgusting smelly pipe was never out of his mouth except when he was eating or swimming. We even began to wonder whether he removed it when he was kissing his betrothed. He gripped the stem of the pipe in the most manly fashion between his strong white teeth and kept it there while talking to you. This annoyed us. Surely it was more polite to take it out and speak properly.

One day, we all went in our little motor-boat to an island we had never been to before, and for once the ancient half-sister and the manly lover decided to come with us. We chose this particular island because we saw some goats on it. They were climbing about on the rocks and we thought it would be fun to go and visit them. But when we landed, we found that the goats were totally wild and we couldn't get near them. So we gave up trying to make friends with them and simply sat around on the smooth rocks in our bathing costumes, enjoying the lovely sun.

The manly lover was filling his pipe. I happened to be watching him as he very carefully packed the tobacco into the bowl from a yellow oilskin pouch. He had just finished doing this and was about to light up when the ancient half-sister called on him to come swimming. So he put down the pipe and off he went.

I stared at the pipe that was lying there on the rocks. About twelve inches away from it, I saw a little heap of dried goat's droppings, each one small and round like a pale brown berry, and at that point, an interesting idea began to sprout in my

People used to think that smoking was beneficial to health. We all now know that it's completely the opposite.

mind. I picked up the pipe and knocked all the tobacco out of it. I then took the goat's droppings and teased them with my fingers until they were nicely shredded. Very gently I poured these shredded droppings into the bowl of the pipe, packing them down with my thumb just as the manly lover always did it. When that was done, I placed a thin layer of real tobacco over the top. The entire family was watching me as I did this. Nobody said a word, but I could sense a glow of approval all round. I replaced the pipe on the rock, and all of us sat back to await the return of the victim. The whole lot of us were in this together now, even my mother. I had drawn them into the plot simply by letting them see what I was doing. It was a silent, rather dangerous family conspiracy.

Back came the manly lover, dripping wet from the sea, chest out, strong and virile, healthy and sunburnt. 'Great swim!' he announced to the world. 'Splendid water! Terrific stuff!' He towelled himself vigorously, making the muscles of his biceps ripple, then he sat down on the rocks and reached for his pipe.

Nine pairs of eyes watched him intently. Nobody giggled to give the game away. We were trembling with anticipation, and a good deal of the suspense was caused by the fact that none of us knew just what was going to happen.

The manly lover put the pipe between his strong white teeth and struck a match. He held the flame over the bowl and sucked. The tobacco ignited and glowed, and the lover's head was enveloped in clouds of blue smoke. 'Ah-h-h,' he said, blowing smoke through his nostrils. 'There's nothing like a good pipe after a bracing swim.'

Still we waited. We could hardly bear the suspense. The sister who was seven couldn't bear it at all. 'What *sort* of

Roald Dahl liked to smoke when he wrote. His writing hut – which remains exactly as he left it – has a ceiling stained yellow by nicotine. And his ashtray is still overflowing with cigarette butts. You can see a replica of his writing hut at the Roald Dahl Museum and Story Centre in Great Missenden.

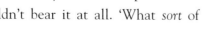

tobacco do you put in that thing?' she asked with superb innocence.

'Navy Cut,' the male lover answered. 'Player's Navy Cut. It's the best there is. These Norwegians use all sorts of disgusting scented tobacco, but I wouldn't touch them.'

'I didn't know they had different tastes,' the small sister went on.

'Of course they do,' the manly lover said. 'All tobaccos are different to the discriminating pipe-smoker. Navy Cut is clean and unadulterated. It's a man's smoke.' The man seemed to go out of his way to use long words like discriminating and unadulterated. We hadn't the foggiest what they meant.

Photograph © Robert Opie

The ancient half-sister, fresh from her swim and now clothed in a towel bathrobe, came and sat herself close to her manly lover. Then the two of them started giving each other those silly little glances and soppy smiles that made us all feel sick. They were far too occupied with one another to notice the awful tension that had settled over our group. They didn't even notice that every face in the crowd was turned towards them. They had sunk once again into their lovers' world where little children did not exist.

The sea was calm, the sun was shining and it was a beautiful day.

Then all of a sudden, the manly lover let out a piercing scream and his whole body shot four feet into the air. His pipe flew out of his mouth and went clattering over the rocks, and the second scream he gave was so shrill and loud that all the seagulls on the island rose up in alarm. His features were twisted like those of a person undergoing severe torture, and his skin had turned the colour of snow. He began spluttering and choking and spewing and hawking and acting generally like a man with some serious internal injury. He was completely speechless.

We stared at him, enthralled.

The ancient half-sister, who must have thought she was about to lose her future husband for ever, was pawing at him and thumping him on the back and crying, 'Darling! Darling! What's happening to you? Where does it hurt? Get the boat! Start the engine! We must rush him to a hospital quickly!' She seemed to have forgotten that there wasn't a hospital within fifty miles.

'I've been poisoned!' spluttered the manly lover. 'It's got into my lungs! It's in my chest! My chest is on fire! My stomach's going up in flames!'

'Help me get him into the boat! Quick!' cried the ancient half-sister, gripping him under the armpits. 'Don't just sit there staring! Come and help!'

'No, no, no!' cried the now not-so-manly lover. 'Leave me alone! I need air! Give me air!' He lay back and breathed in deep draughts of splendid Norwegian ocean air, and in another minute or so, he was sitting up again and was on the way to recovery.

'What in the world came over you?' asked the ancient half-sister, clasping his hands tenderly in hers.

'I can't imagine,' he murmured. 'I simply can't imagine.'

Roald Dahl liked to play tricks all his life. One of his favourite practical jokes was decanting cheap plonk into empty wine bottles of an excellent vintage. He loved to watch his guests' reactions when they drank it.

His face was as still and white as virgin snow and his hands were trembling. 'There must be a reason for it,' he added. 'There's got to be a reason.'

'I know the reason!' shouted the seven-year-old sister, screaming with laughter. 'I know what it was!'

'What was it?' snapped the ancient one. 'What have you been up to? Tell me at once!'

'It's his pipe!' shouted the small sister, still convulsed with laughter.

'What's wrong with my pipe?' said the manly lover.

'You've been smoking goat's tobacco!' cried the small sister.

It took a few moments for the full meaning of these words to dawn upon the two lovers, but when it did, and when the terrible anger began to show itself on the manly lover's face, and when he started to rise slowly and menacingly to his feet, we all sprang up and ran for our lives and jumped off the rocks into the deep water.

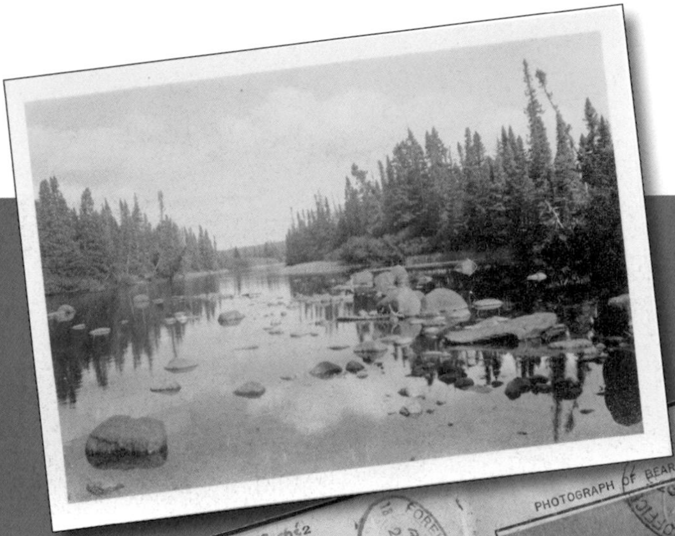

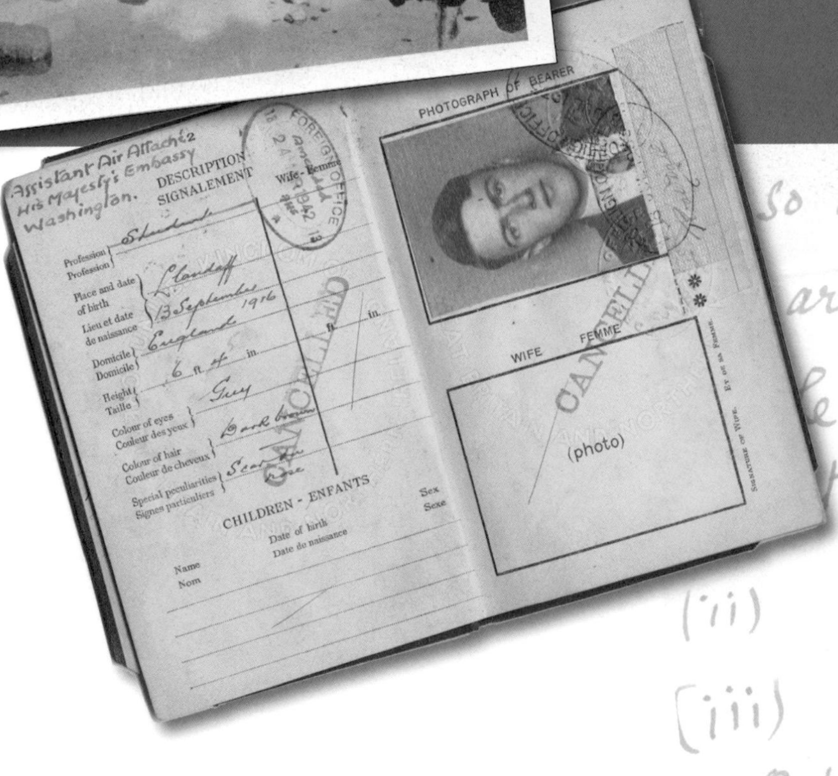

P. S. I have'nt

Porta varat culpa

Assistant Air Attaché
His Majesty's Embassy
Washington.

PHOTOGRAPH OF BEARER

DESCRIPTION
SIGNALEMENT

Profession
Profession — Student

Place and date
of birth
Lieu et date
de naissance — Llandaff 13 September 1916

Domicile
Domicile — England

Height
Taille — 6 ft 4 in.

Colour of eyes
Couleur des yeux — Grey

Colour of hair
Couleur de cheveux — Dark brown

Special peculiarities
Signes particuliers — Scar

CHILDREN - ENFANTS

Sex
Sexe

Name
Nom

Date of birth
Date de naissance

WIFE   FEMME

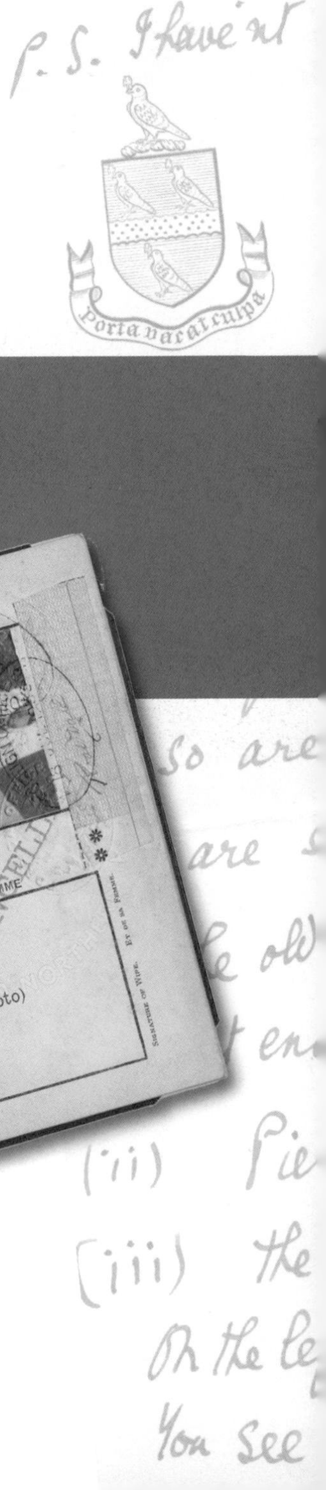

(photo)

so are
are s
e old
t en

(ii) Pie

(iii) the

On the le
You see

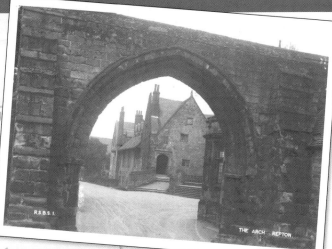

Swimming Bath, Repton School.

Repton and Shell 1929-36
(age 13-20)

Prunes.

more photos.

...ry. I am going to...

... & hang it in my r...

...lool.

...SS. Is'nt it a funny one.

...u can see Sisters Cairn," Hay-miss...

...s just cracked a joke with her,

THE PRIORY HOUSE,
REPTON,
DERBY.

Dear Mama

Thanks awfully for the parcel and your letters. We had a great supper last night. We fried the sausages and poured hieny beans over them. then we had force & cream. Those biscuits are awfully good. Last night we had a heavy snowfall, and there is about ... of snow on the ground. Macdonald & I ... Tobogganing

Love from

Roald

On ship To Newfoundland

photography at Repton

Roald Dahl left St Peter's in 1929, and started at Repton after the Christmas holidays – in January 1930.

Getting dressed for the big school

When I was twelve, my mother said to me, 'I've entered you for Marlborough and Repton. Which would you like to go to?'

Both were famous Public Schools, but that was all I knew about them. 'Repton,' I said. 'I'll go to Repton.' It was an easier word to say than Marlborough.

'Very well,' my mother said. 'You shall go to Repton.'

We were living in Kent then, in a place called Bexley. Repton was up in the Midlands, near Derby, and some 140 miles away to the north. That was of no consequence. There were plenty of trains. Nobody was taken to school by car in those days. We were put on the train.

alfhild, me, asta, Else and dogs. Tenby.

Repton had been educating pupils for quite some time before Roald Dahl arrived – 372 years, to be precise. And it's still going strong.

I was exactly thirteen in September 1929 when the time came for me to go to Repton. On the day of my departure, I had first of all to get dressed for the part. I had been to London with my mother the week before to buy the school clothes, and I remember how shocked I was when I saw the outfit I was expected to wear.

'I can't possibly go about in *those*!' I cried. 'Nobody wears things like that!'

'Are you sure you haven't made a mistake?' my mother said to the shop assistant.

'If he's going to Repton, madam, he must wear these clothes,' the assistant said firmly.

And now this amazing fancy-dress was all laid out on my bed waiting to be put on. 'Put it on,' my mother said. 'Hurry up or you'll miss the train.'

'I'll look like a complete idiot,' I said. My mother went out of the room and left me to it. With immense reluctance, I began to dress myself.

First there was a white shirt with a detachable white collar. This collar was unlike any other collar I had seen. It was as stiff as a piece of perspex. At the front, the stiff points of the collar were bent over to make a pair of wings, and the whole thing was so tall that the points of the wings, as I discovered later, rubbed against the underneath of my chin. It was known as a butterfly collar.

To attach the butterfly collar to the shirt you needed a back stud and a front stud. I had never been through this rigmarole before. I must do this properly, I told myself. So first I put the back stud into the back of the collar-band of the shirt. Then I tried to attach the back of the collar to the back stud, but the collar was so stiff I couldn't get the stud through the slit. I decided to soften it with spit. I put the edge of the collar into my mouth and sucked the starch away. It worked. The stud went through the slit and the back of the collar was now attached to the back of the shirt.

Roald Dahl wears his boater while at Repton School

I inserted the front stud into one side of the front of the shirt and slipped the shirt over my head. With the help of a mirror, I now set about pushing the top of the front stud through the first of the two slits in the front of the collar. It wouldn't go. The slit was so small and stiff and starchy that nothing would go through it. I took the shirt off and put both the front slits of the collar into my mouth and chewed them until they were soft. The starch didn't taste of anything. I put the shirt back on again and at last I was able to get the front stud through the collar-slits.

Around the collar but underneath the butterfly wings, I tied a black tie, using an ordinary tie-knot.

Dear mama
Thanks for your letter.
I mean half a dozen Van Heusen Collars. not Shirts.
Love from
Roald.

Then came the trousers and the braces. The trousers were black with thin pinstriped grey lines running down them. I buttoned the braces on to the trousers, six buttons in all, then I put on the trousers and adjusted the braces to the correct length by sliding two brass clips up and down.

I put on a brand new pair of black shoes and laced them up.

Now for the waistcoat. This was also black and it had twelve buttons down the front and two little waistcoat pockets on either side, one above the other. I put it on and did up the buttons, starting at the top and working down. I was glad

Today younger pupils at Repton wear a much simpler uniform: school blazer, dark grey trousers or skirt – the school now admits girls as well as boys – white shirt or blouse, V-neck pullover and black, polished, leather shoes.

I didn't have to chew each of those button-holes to get the buttons through them.

All this was bad enough for a boy who had never before worn anything more elaborate than a pair of shorts and a blazer. But the jacket put the lid on it. It wasn't actually a jacket, it was a sort of tail-coat, and it was without a doubt the most ridiculous garment I had ever seen. Like the waistcoat, it was jet black and made of a heavy serge-like material. In the front it was cut away so that the two sides met only at one point, about halfway down the waistcoat. Here there was a single button and this had to be done up.

From the button downwards, the lines of the coat separated and curved away behind the legs of the wearer and came together again at the backs of the knees, forming a pair of 'tails'. These tails were separated by a slit and when you walked about they flapped against your legs. I put the thing on and did up the front button. Feeling like an undertaker's apprentice in a funeral parlour, I crept downstairs.

My sisters shrieked with laughter when I appeared. 'He can't go out in *those*!' they cried. 'He'll be arrested by the police!'

'Put your hat on,' my mother said, handing me a stiff wide-brimmed straw-hat with a blue and black band around it. I put it on and did my best to look dignified. The sisters fell all over the room laughing.

the hat-band being & something like this: ___, the white stripes are realy blue, and the bit filled in is black. p. th

My mother got me out of the house before I lost my nerve completely and together we walked through the village to Bexley station. My mother was going to accompany me to London and see me on to the Derby train, but she had been told that on no account should she travel farther than that. I had only a small suitcase to carry. My trunk had been sent on ahead labelled 'Luggage in Advance'.

'Nobody's taking the slightest notice of you,' my mother said as we walked through Bexley High Street.

And curiously enough nobody was.

'I have learnt one thing about England,' my mother went on. 'It is a country where men love to wear uniforms and eccentric clothes. Two hundred years ago their clothes were even more eccentric then they are today. You can consider yourself lucky you don't have to wear a wig on your head and ruffles on your sleeves.'

Bexley High Street.

Public school is anything but that. Although it might sound as if it's open to the general public, 'public' refers to schools named in the **Public Schools Act 1868**. These schools receive all their **funding** from **private sources**, rather than from the state or the government and now prefer to be called **independent** rather than public.

'I still feel an ass,' I said.

'Everyone who looks at you,' my mother said, 'knows that you are going away to a Public School. All English Public Schools have their own different crazy uniforms. People will be thinking how lucky you are to be going to one of those famous places.'

We took the train from Bexley to Charing Cross and then went by taxi to Euston Station. At Euston, I was put on the train for Derby with a lot of other boys who all wore the same ridiculous clothes as me, and away I went.

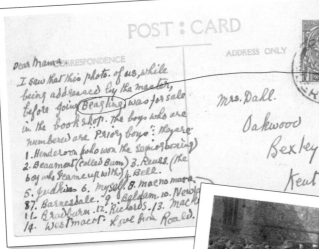

POST · CARD

CORRESPONDENCE

Dear Mama
I saw that this photo. of us, while being addressed by the master, before going Beagling *was for sale in the bookshop. the boys who are numbered are Priory boys": they are*
1. Henderson (who won the senior boxing)
2. Beaumont (called Bum) 3. Reuss. (the boy who I came up with) 4. Bell.
5. Judkins 6. myself 8. macnamara.
87. Barnesdale. 9. Baldam. 10. Newe
11. Bradburn. 12. Richards. 13. mach
14. Westmacot. Love from Roald.

ADDRESS ONLY

Mrs. Dahl.
Oakwood
Bexley
Kent.

'Beagling' is hunting of hares or foxes using **beagles** – dogs with an exceedingly good sense of smell.

While at Repton, Roald Dahl lived in the **Priory House**. But a house was much more than a place to live – it was a **team** too. Everything you did at school was as part of that team.

Beagling, Repton 1930.

Boazers

At Repton, prefects were never called prefects. They were called Boazers, and they had the power of life and death over us junior boys. They could summon us down in our pyjamas at night-time and thrash us for leaving just one football sock on the floor of the changing-room when it should have been hung up on a peg. A Boazer could thrash us for a hundred and one other piddling little misdemeanours – for burning his toast at tea-time, for failing to dust his study properly, for failing to get his study fire burning in spite of spending half your pocket money on fire-lighters, for being late at roll-call, for talking in evening Prep, for forgetting to change into house-shoes at six o'clock. The list was endless.

'Four with the dressing-gown on or three with it off?' the Boazer would say to you in the changing-room late at night.

Others in the dormitory had told you what to answer to this question. 'Four with it on,' you mumbled, trembling.

This Boazer was famous for the speed of his strokes. Most of them paused between each stroke to prolong the operation, but Williamson, the great footballer, cricketer and athlete, always delivered his strokes in a series of swift back and forth movements without any pause between them at all. Four strokes would rain down upon your bottom so

Boazer wasn't a real word. It was Roald Dahl's way of spelling 'Beausieur', which means 'smart young man' in French.

Later Roald became a **footballer** (he's in the front row on the far left) but *never* a Boazer.

167

fast that it was all over in four seconds.

A ritual took place in the dormitory after each beating. The victim was required to stand in the middle of the room and lower his pyjama trousers so that the damage could be inspected. Half a dozen experts would crowd round you and express their opinions in highly professional language.

'*What* a super job.'

'He's got *every single* one in the same place!'

'Crikey! Nobody could tell you had more than *one*, except for the mess!'

'Boy, that Williamson's got a *terrific* eye!'

'*Of course* he's got a terrific eye! Why d'you think he's a Cricket Teamer?'

'There's no wet blood though! If you had had just one more he'd have got some blood out!'

'Through a *dressing-gown*, too! It's pretty amazing, isn't it!'

'Most Boazers couldn't get a result like that *without* a dressing-gown!'

'You must have tremendously thin skin! Even Williamson couldn't have done that to *ordinary* skin!'

'Did he use the long one or the short one?'

'Hang *on*! Don't pull them up yet! I've got to see this again!'

And I would stand there, slightly bemused by this cool clinical approach. Once, I was still standing in the middle of the dormitory with my pyjama trousers around my knees when Williamson came through the door. 'What on earth do you think you're doing?' he said, knowing very well exactly what I was doing.

'N-nothing,' I stammered. 'N-nothing at all.'

'Pull those pyjamas up and get into bed immediately!' he ordered, but I noticed that as he turned away to go out of the door, he craned his head ever so slightly to one side to catch a glimpse of my bare bottom and his own handiwork. I was certain I detected a little glimmer of pride around the edges of his mouth before he closed the door behind him.

Painful Punishments

At my last boarding school there were at least one hundred different diabolical punishments. But that was more than fifty years ago and things have changed a lot since then. We got punished for burning the prefect's toast or if he found a speck of dust on a shelf in his study, or for not touching the rims of our straw hats as we passed a master on the road, or not taking them off if we passed a master's wife. We got punished for leaving games clothes on the floor of the changing-room, for being late for anything at all, for talking in class, or if the brass buttons on our OTC uniforms were not shining like gold.

Above all, we were punished for poor work. But the master for whom one did the bad work never did the punishing. That pleasure was reserved for one's Housemaster. A rather subtle method was employed by which the form-master told the Housemaster of your misdemeanour. The form-master would say in class, 'Dahl, take eighty blue', or 'one hundred and twenty blue' or whatever. 'Blue' was a special kind of blue paper which only

The OTC stands for the **Officers' Training Corps** and is part of the British Army, providing military training to school and university students.

the Housemaster possessed, and each large page contained forty lines. You therefore had to go to your Housemaster to get it. After lunch every day, there was a queue of boys in the Housemaster's study drawing out small fractions of their pocket-money which they had deposited with him at the beginning of term. We always paid in two and drew it out in tiny little bits at a time – thruppence, sixpence or a shilling. A boy who had been given 'blue' would go to the end of this queue so that when his time came he would be alone with the Housemaster. He would then be cross-examined, often beaten. Two hundred and forty blue, the maximum, was an automatic and severe thrashing. He would then have to go off and fill in all those two hundred and forty lines with an original composition of his own. Whatever other work he had to do or games he had to play, 'blue' had to be completed and delivered by hand to the form-master (often a mile away) before lock-up on that same day. Two-forty blue is three thousand words. That's quite a lot to do in your spare time in one afternoon. But do it you had to, and do it you did.

This letter from Roald Dahl to his mother accompanied a series of photos that he'd taken. He was very fond of photography.

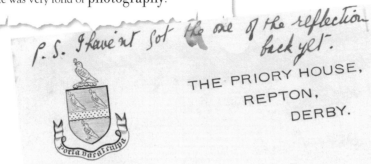

P.S. I haven't got the one of the reflection back yet.

THE PRIORY HOUSE,
REPTON,
DERBY.

Porta vacat culpa

'cake'

'prunes'

Roald Dahl's mother still sent him food parcels . . .

'BOSS'

The Headmaster was known to all the boys as 'the boss'.

Dear Mama

Thanks frightfully for the Parcel, it was a jolly heavy one. the cake is fine, and so are the Prunes.

Here are some more photos.

(i) the old Priory. I am going to have that enlarged, & hang it in my room.

(ii) Piers School.

(iii) the BOSS. Is'nt it a funny one. On the left you can see Sisters Cairn, "Hay, mis's". You see he has just cracked a joke with her, and at the very moment, he did'nt know he was being taken. I'm very proud of it.

The Headmaster

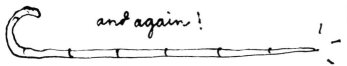

and again!

The Headmaster, while I was at Repton, struck me as being a rather shoddy bandy-legged little fellow with a big bald head and lots of energy but not much charm. Mind you, I never did know him well because in all those months and years I was at the school, I doubt whether he addressed more than six sentences to me altogether. So perhaps it was wrong of me to form a judgement like that.

What is so interesting about this Headmaster is that he became a famous person later on. At the end of my third year, he was suddenly appointed Bishop of Chester and off he went to live in a palace by the River Dee. I remember at the time trying to puzzle out how on earth a person could suddenly leap from being a schoolmaster to becoming a Bishop all in one jump, but there were bigger puzzles to come.

From Chester, he was soon promoted again to become Bishop of London, and from there, after not all that many years, he bounced up the ladder once more to get the top job of them all, Archbishop of Canterbury! And not long after that it was he himself who had the task of crowning our present Queen in Westminster Abbey with half the world watching him on television. Well, well, well! And this was the man who

This Headmaster's name was Geoffrey Fisher. He was Head of Repton School until July 1932.

In 1932, while Roald Dahl was at Repton, a very important person was born 120 miles away in Sidcup. This was Quentin Blake – Whitbread Award winner, illustrator of over 300 children's books and author and illustrator of over 30 more. But most importantly, he illustrated Roald Dahl's books, bringing the BFG, Matilda, Willy Wonka and many more unforgettable characters to life in a totally unique and quite brilliant way.

This is J. T. Christie, Headmaster of Repton from 1932 to 1937.

used to deliver the most vicious beatings to the boys under his care!

By now I am sure you will be wondering why I lay so much emphasis upon school beatings in these pages. The answer is that I cannot help it. All through my school life I was appalled by the fact that masters and senior boys were allowed literally to wound other boys, and sometimes quite severely. I couldn't get over it. I never have got over it. It would, of course, be unfair to suggest that *all* masters were constantly beating the daylights out of *all* the boys in those days. They weren't. Only a few did so, but that was quite enough to leave a lasting impression of horror upon me. It left another more physical impression upon me as well. Even today, whenever I have to sit for any length of time on a hard bench or chair, I begin to feel my heart beating along the old lines that the cane made on my bottom some fifty-five years ago.

There is nothing wrong with a few quick sharp tickles on the rump. They probably do a naughty boy a lot of good. But this Headmaster we were talking about wasn't just tickling you when he took out his cane to deliver a flogging. He never flogged me, thank goodness, but I was given a vivid description of one of these ceremonies by my best friend at Repton, whose name was Michael. Michael was ordered to take down his trousers and kneel on the Headmaster's sofa with the top half of his body hanging over one end of the sofa. The great man then gave him one terrific crack. After that, there was a pause. The cane was put down and the Headmaster began filling his pipe from a tin of tobacco. He also started to lecture the kneeling boy about sin and wrongdoing. Soon, the cane was picked up again and a second tremendous crack was administered upon the trembling buttocks. Then the pipe-filling business and the lecture went on for maybe another thirty seconds. Then came the third crack of the cane. Then the instrument of torture was put once more upon the table and a box of matches was produced. A match was struck and applied to the pipe. The pipe failed to light properly. A fourth stroke was delivered, with the lecture continuing. This slow and fearsome process went on until ten terrible strokes had been delivered, and all the time, over the pipe-lighting and the match-striking, the lecture on evil and wrongdoing and sinning and misdeeds and malpractice went on without a stop. It even went on as the strokes were being administered. At the end of it all, a basin, a sponge and a small clean towel were produced by the Headmaster, and the victim was told to wash away the blood before pulling up his trousers.

Do you wonder then that this man's behaviour used to puzzle me tremendously? He was an ordinary clergyman at that time as well as being Headmaster, and I would sit in the dim light of the school chapel and listen to him preaching about the Lamb of God and about Mercy and Forgiveness and all the rest of it and my young mind would become totally confused. I knew very well that only the night before this preacher had shown neither Forgiveness nor Mercy in flogging some small boy who had broken the rules.

So what was it all about? I used to ask myself.

Did they preach one thing and practise another, these men of God?

And if someone had told me at the time that this flogging clergyman was one day to become the Archbishop of Canterbury, I would never have believed it.

It was all this, I think, that made me begin to have doubts about religion and even about God. If this person, I kept telling myself, was one of God's chosen salesmen on earth, then there must be something very wrong about the whole business.

Mr S. S. Jenkyns, the Housemaster of Priory House, known as 'Binks'. He was very keen on sport and anxious for Priory House to win!

These are the reports **Roald Dahl** mentions. Although he certainly wasn't **top** of the class, he doesn't seem to have been at the **bottom** of the class either!

'I have never met anyone who so persistently wrote words meaning the exact opposite of what he obviously intended'

'Better lately'

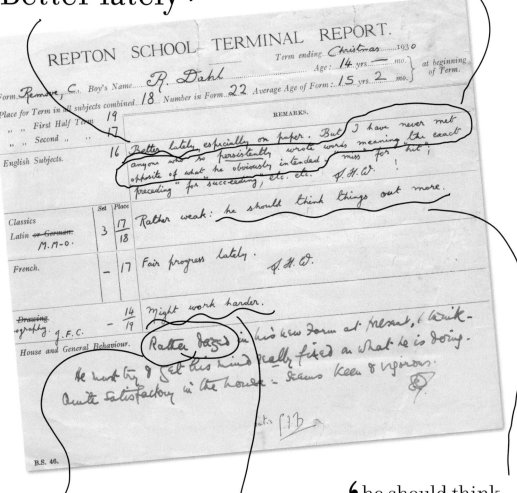

REPTON SCHOOL TERMINAL REPORT.

Term ending Christmas 1930

Form Remove C. Boy's Name R. Dahl. Age: 14 yrs. — mo. } at beginning
18 Number in Form 22 Average Age of Form: 15 yrs. 2 mo. } of Term.

Place for Term in all subjects combined 18

First Half Term	19	
Second ,, ,,	17	
English Subjects.	16	Better lately, especially on paper. But I have never met anyone who so persistently wrote words meaning the exact opposite of what he obviously intended ; "miss" for "hit"; "preceding" for "succeeding", etc. etc. J. H. W. !

REMARKS.

	Set	Place	
Classics			
Latin or German: M.M-O.	3	17 / 18	Rather weak : he should think things out more.
French.	—	17	Fair progress lately. J. H. W.
Drawing. ography. J.F.C.	—	14 / 19	Might work harder.
House and General Behaviour.			Rather dazed in his new form at present, I think — He must try & get his mind really fixed on what he is doing. Quite satisfactory in the house — Seems keen & vigorous.

B.S. 46.

'Rather dazed'

'Might work harder'

'he should think things out more'

'ideas limited'

'Consistently idle: too pleased with himself'

REPTON SCHOOL TERMINAL REPORT.

Form... R^a ... Boy's Name... R. Dahl ... Term ending... July 26 1932

Place for Term in all subjects combined 12 ... Number in Form 12 ... Average Age of Form: 16 yrs. 9 mo. ... Age: 15 yrs. 5 mo. ... at beginning of Term.

" " First Half Term 12
" " Second " 12

REMARKS.

English Subjects.

Hist. 6. Has done better this term: his work has sometimes been really good. PHB.

Engl. Satisfactory work (ideas limited.) RCB.

Geog. Consistently idle: too pleased with himself. WJS.

Classics Latin or German. Set II Place — Satisfactory progress for me. m.MB.

French. 12. During the 2nd half term he has produced better results. there is little doubt but that he often tries to hide idleness behind a veil of stupidity. his own growth may perhaps excuse some of his apathy. SY.

Drawing.

House and General Behaviour. He is so large that it is often difficult to remember how young he is. It is time however that he put more effort into his heart: he is capable of doing quite respectable work.

B.S. 46.

He ... not the best he could produce by a good way ...

'He is so large that it is often difficult to remember how young he is'

'he often tries to hide idleness behind a veil of stupidity...'

Chocolates

Every now and again, a plain grey cardboard box was dished out to each boy in our House, and this, believe it or not, was a present from the great chocolate manufacturers, Cadbury. Inside the box there were twelve bars of chocolate, all of different shapes, all with different fillings and all with numbers from one to twelve stamped on the chocolate underneath. Eleven of these bars were new inventions from the factory. The twelfth was the 'control' bar, one that we all knew well, usually a Cadbury's Coffee Cream bar. Also in the box was a sheet of paper with the numbers one to twelve on it as well as two blank columns, one for giving marks to each chocolate from nought to ten, and the other for comments.

All we were required to do in return for this splendid gift was to taste very carefully each bar of chocolate, give it marks and make an intelligent comment on why we liked it or disliked it.

It was a clever stunt. Cadbury's were using some of the greatest chocolate-bar experts in the world to test out their new inventions. We were of a sensible age, between thirteen and eighteen, and we knew intimately every chocolate bar in existence, from the Milk Flake to the Lemon Marshmallow. Quite obviously our opinions on anything new would be valuable. All of us entered into this game with great gusto,

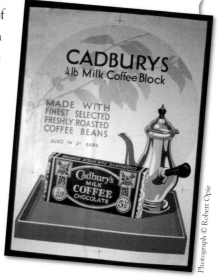

Photograph © Robert Opie

As far as Roald Dahl was concerned, the years 1930 to 1937 were quite the most important time in the history of chocolate:

'In the seven years of this glorious and golden decade, all the great classic chocolate bars were invented: the Crunchie, the Whole-Nut Bar, the Mars Bar, the Black Magic Assortment, Tiffin, Caramello, Aero, Malteser, Quality Street Assortment, Kit Kat, Rolo and Smarties.

In music the equivalent would be the golden age when compositions by Bach and Mozart and Beethoven were given to us.

In painting it was the equivalent of the Renaissance in Italian art and the advent of the Impressionists towards the end of the nineteenth century.

In literature it was Tolstoy and Balzac and Dickens.

I tell you, there has been nothing like it in the history of chocolate and there never will be.'
(The Roald Dahl Cookbook)

sitting in our studies and nibbling each bar with the air of connoisseurs, giving our marks and making our comments. 'Too subtle for the common palate,' was one note that I remember writing down.

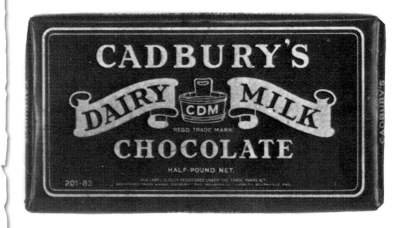

For me, the importance of all this was that I began to realize that the large chocolate companies actually did possess inventing rooms and they took their inventing very seriously. I used to picture a long white room like a laboratory with pots of chocolate and fudge and all sorts of other delicious fillings bubbling away on the stoves, while men and women in white coats moved between the bubbling pots, tasting and mixing and concocting their wonderful new inventions. I used to imagine myself working in one of these labs and suddenly I would come up with something so absolutely unbearably delicious that I would grab it in my hand and go rushing out of the lab and along the corridor and right into the office of the great Mr Cadbury himself. 'I've got it, sir!' I would shout, putting the chocolate in front of him. 'It's fantastic! It's fabulous! It's marvellous! It's irresistible!'

Slowly, the great man would pick up my newly invented

chocolate and he would take a small bite. He would roll it round his mouth. Then all at once, he would leap up from his chair, crying, 'You've got it! You've done it! It's a miracle!' He would slap me on the back and shout, 'We'll sell it by the million! We'll sweep the world with this one! How on earth did you do it? Your salary is doubled!'

It was lovely dreaming those dreams, and I have no doubt at all that, thirty-five years later, when I was looking for a plot for my second book for children, I remembered those little cardboard boxes and the newly invented chocolates inside them, and I began to write a book called *Charlie and the Chocolate Factory*.

Saturday, first I broke it in half, and only half came out, then the other bit came out, it was my dog tooth, and it was a very bad one, I am glad it came out. Will you please send me a few sweets because we had none, last week, I am sorry my writing is so untidy, but I have not much time on week days.

'This is *Charlie. How d'you do*? And how d'you do? And how d'you do again? He is pleased to meet you.' And so begins one of the most famous – and most chocolatey – adventures . . .

Ten Horrid Little Boys and Girls

Charlie and the Chocolate Factory took me a terrible long time to write. The first time I did it, I got everything wrong. I wrote a story about a little boy who was going round a chocolate factory and he accidentally fell into a big tub of melted chocolate and got sucked into the machine that made chocolate figures and he couldn't get out. It was a splendid big chocolate figure, a chocolate boy the same size as him. And it was Easter time, and the figure was put in a shop window, and in the end a lady came in and bought it as an Easter present for her little girl, and carried it home. On Easter Day, the little girl opened the box with her present in it, and took it out and then she decided to eat some of it. She would start with the head, she thought. So she broke off the nose, and when she saw a real human nose sticking out underneath and too big bright human eyes staring at her through the eye-holes in the chocolate, she got a nasty shock. And so it went on.

But the story wasn't good enough. I rewrote it, and rewrote it, and the little tentacles kept shooting out from my head, searching for new ideas, and at last one of them came back with Mr Willy Wonka and his marvellous chocolate factory and then came Charlie and his parents and grandparents and the Golden Tickets and the nasty children, Violet Beauregarde and Veruca Salt and all the rest of them.

As a matter of fact, I got so wrapped up in all those nasty children, and they made me giggle so much that I couldn't stop inventing them. In the first full version of 'Charlie and the Chocolate Factory', I had no less than ten horrid little boys and girls. That was too many. It became confusing. It wasn't a good book. But I liked them all so much, I didn't want to take any of them out.

One of them, who was taken out in the end was a horrid little girl who was disgustingly rude to her parents and also thoroughly disobedient. Her name was Miranda Mary Piker. And I remember she fell into a machine that made peanut-brittle. And at the end of it all the Oompa-Loompas sang this song (which never appeared in the book):

Oh Miranda Mary Piker
Now could anybody like her,
Such a rude and disobedient little kid.
So we said why don't we fix her
In the peanut-brittle mixer.
Then we're sure to like her better than we did.
Soon this child who was so vicious
Will have gotten quite delicious,
And her father will have surely understood,
That instead of saying, 'Miranda, oh the beast I cannot stand her',
He'll be saying, 'Oh, how luscious and how good!'

These **lucky characters** did make it into the final draft of *Charlie and the Chocolate Factory*.

VERUCA SALT   MIKE TEAVEE   AUGUSTUS GLOOP   VIOLET BEUREGUARDE

Corkers

There were about thirty or more masters at Repton and most of them were amazingly dull and totally colourless and completely uninterested in boys. But Corkers, an eccentric old bachelor, was neither dull nor colourless. Corkers was a charmer, a vast ungainly man with drooping bloodhound cheeks and filthy clothes. He wore creaseless flannel trousers and a brown tweed jacket with patches all over it and bits of dried food on the lapels. He was meant to teach us mathematics, but in truth he taught us nothing at all and that was the way he meant it to be. His lessons consisted of an endless series of distractions all invented by him so that the subject of mathematics would never have to be discussed. He would come lumbering into the classroom and sit down at his desk and glare at the class. We would wait expectantly, wondering what was coming next.

Major Noel Strickland (also known as 'Strickers' or 'Corkers').

'Let's have a look at the crossword puzzle in today's *Times*,' he would say, fishing a crumpled newspaper out of his jacket pocket. 'That'll be a lot more fun than fiddling around with figures. I hate figures. Figures are probably the dreariest things on this earth.'

'Then why do you teach mathematics, sir?' somebody asked him.

'I don't,' he said, smiling slyly. 'I only *pretend* to teach it.'

Corkers would proceed to draw the framework of the

crossword on the blackboard and we would all spend the rest of the lesson trying to solve it while he read out the clues. We enjoyed that.

The only time I can remember him vaguely touching upon mathematics was when he whisked a square of tissue-paper out of his pocket and waved it around. 'Look at this,' he said. 'This tissue-paper is one-hundredth of an inch thick. I fold it once, making it double. I fold it again, making it four thicknesses. Now then, I will give a large bar of Cadbury's Fruit and Nut Milk Chocolate to any boy who can tell me, to the nearest twelve inches, how thick it will be if I fold it fifty times.'

We all stuck up our hands and started guessing. 'Twenty-four inches, sir' . . . 'Three feet, sir' . . . 'Five yards, sir' . . . 'Three inches, sir.'

'You're not very clever, are you,' Corkers said. 'The answer is the distance from the earth to the sun. That's how thick it would be.' We were enthralled by this piece of intelligence and asked him to prove it on the blackboard, which he did.

Another time, he brought a two-foot-long grass-snake into class and insisted that every boy should handle it in order to cure us for ever, as he said, of a fear of snakes. This caused quite a commotion.

Corkers

I cannot remember all the other thousands of splendid things that old Corkers cooked up to keep his class happy, but there was one that I shall never forget which was repeated at intervals of about three weeks throughout each term. He would be talking to us about this or that when suddenly he would stop in mid-sentence and a look of intense pain would cloud his ancient countenance. Then his head would come up and his great nose would begin to sniff the air and he would cry aloud, 'By God! This is too much! This is going too far! This is intolerable!'

Thanks awfully for the Tablets. I took some a few times and the indigestion has stopped now, they are jolly good

We knew exactly what was coming next, but we always played along with him. 'What's the matter, sir? What's happened? Are you all right, sir? Are you feeling ill?'

Up went the great nose once again, and the head would move slowly from side to side and the nose would sniff the air delicately as though searching for a leak of gas or the smell of something burning. 'This is not to be tolerated!' he would cry. 'This is *unbearable*!'

'But what's the *matter*, sir?'

'I'll tell you what's the matter,' Corkers would shout. 'Somebody's *farted*!'

'Oh no, sir!' . . . 'Not me, sir!' . . . 'Nor me, sir!' . . . 'It's none of us, sir!'

At this point, he would rise majestically to his feet and call out at the top of his voice, '*Use door as fan! Open all windows!*'

Here's another of Roald Dahl's **favourite facts**:

'You each have or had *four grandparents*. Taking *each generation* as *thirty years* you can easily prove that back in the *fifteenth century* you had about *eight million direct ancestors*. This was more that the *entire population of Britain* at that time. Therefore, everyone was your own direct ancestor. *Chaucer* and *Shakespeare* must have been one of your *great great grandparents*. And I've never been able to find out why this isn't really true although the arithmetic proves it.'

This was the signal for frantic activity and everyone in the class would leap to his feet. It was a well-rehearsed operation and each of us knew exactly what he had to do. Four boys would man the door and begin swinging it back and forth at great speed. The rest would start clambering about on the gigantic windows which occupied one whole wall of the room, flinging the lower ones open, using a long pole with a hook on the end to open the top ones, and leaning out to gulp the fresh air in mock distress. While this was going on, Corkers himself would march serenely out of the room, muttering, 'It's the cabbage that does it! All they give you is disgusting cabbage and Brussels sprouts and you go off like fire-crackers!' And that was the last we saw of Corkers for the day.

The **school shop** at Repton was known as 'the Grubber'. Recognize the name? Roald Dahl used it for the sweetshop in *The Giraffe and the Pelly and Me*. But unlike the shop in the story, the Grubber at Repton sold everything from **sweets** to **cricket shoes**.

School dinners!

The boys at Repton were allowed to cook for themselves – and here are just some of the letters in which Roald Dahl describes what he liked to eat . . .

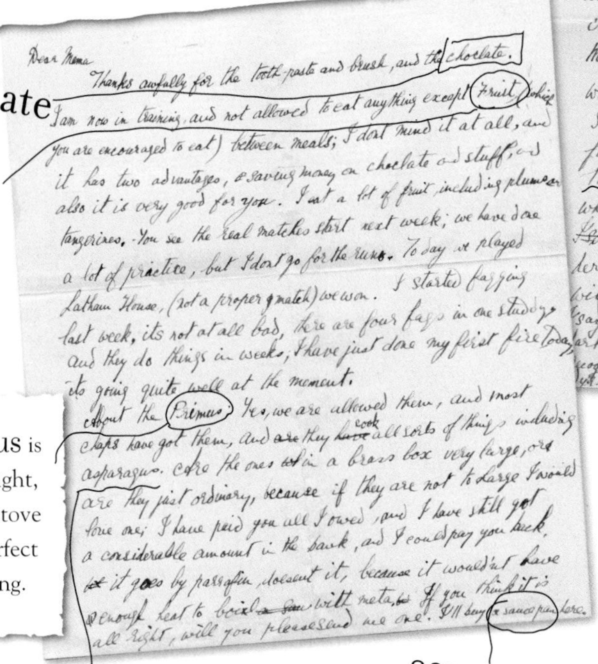

chocolate

fruit

A Primus is a lightweight, portable stove that is perfect for camping.

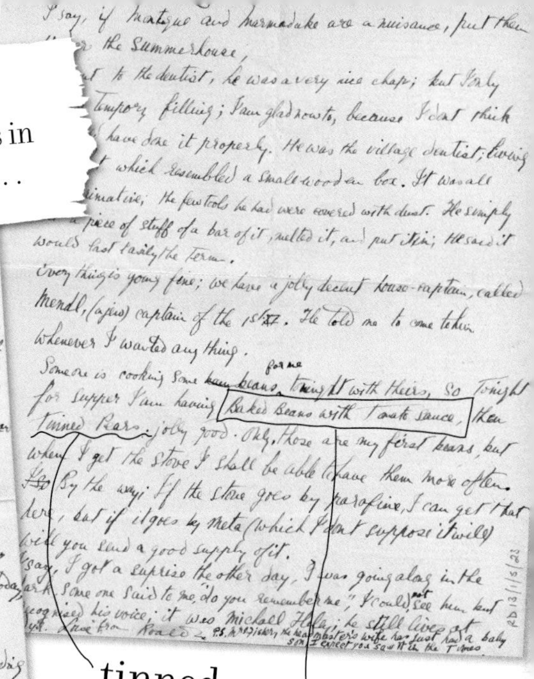

asparagus

saucepan

tinned pears

baked beans with tomato sauce

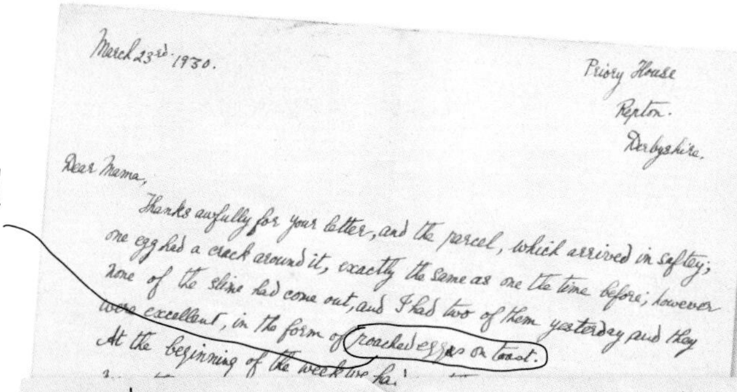

poached eggs on toast

magnesia pills

. . . and after all this food, it's not surprising he had indigestion!

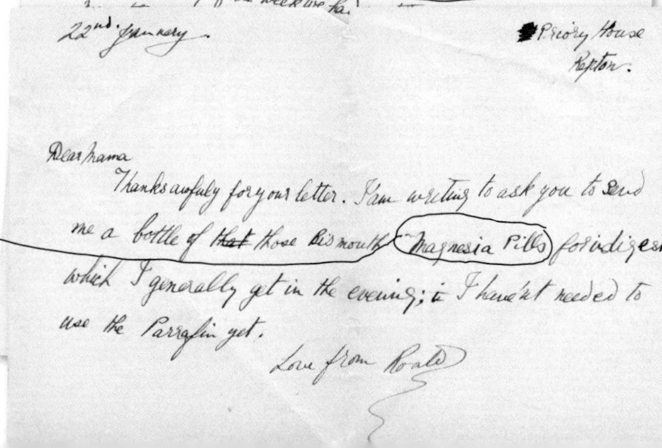

Mr and Mrs Jenkyns with their family and the boys from Priory House.
Roald Dahl is on the far right of the second row from the front.

Fagging

I spent two long years as a Fag at Repton, which meant I was the servant of the studyholder in whose study I had my little desk. If the studyholder happened to be a House Boazer, so much the worse for me because Boazers were a dangerous breed. During my second term, I was unfortunate enough to be put into the study of the Head of the House, a supercilious and obnoxious seventeen-year-old called Carleton. Carleton always looked at you right down the length of his nose, and

even if you were as tall as him, which I happened to be, he would tilt his head back and still manage to look at you down the length of his nose. Carleton had three Fags in his study and all of us were terrified of him, especially on Sunday mornings, because Sunday was study-cleaning time. All the Fags in all the studies had to take off their jackets, roll up their sleeves, fetch buckets and floor-cloths and get down to cleaning out their studyholder's study. And when I say cleaning out, I mean

The Priory.

JANUARY, 1930.

VI.	J. F. MENDL
VI.2	Westerberg
V2	K. J. Mendl
VI 2	Boddam-Whetham
	E. K. Lee
J. D. N. C. Henderson	
V.I	R. G. Beldam
	I. D. MacDonald
	M. M. Wilson
	Bell
	Middleton
	Ross Taylor
V2	Arnold
	Muller
	Furse
	Higgins
P. A. Brown	
	Richards
	Ommanney
	Kelsey
	MacBrayne
	A. C. Mackay
	Sherston
R	W. Wilson
	Clyde-Smith
	Dean
	Llewelyn
	Judkins
	Bradburn
	Barclay
	I. B. Mackay
	Westmacott
IV.I	Newland
	I. D. Dunlop
	K. F. Macdonald
	A. A. Wilson
	B. L. L. Reuss
	A. J. L. Reuss
	Barnsdale
IV.2	P. E. L. Beldam
	D. F. Mendl
	T. S. Smith
	Macnamara
	C. D. Beaumont
	Turton
	Ashton
	Dahl

Can you find Roald Dahl's name on the register for 1930?

practically sterilizing the place. We scrubbed the floor and washed the windows and polished the grate and dusted the ledges and wiped the picture-frames and carefully tidied away all the hockey-sticks and cricket-bats and umbrellas.

All that Sunday morning we had been slogging away cleaning Carleton's study, and then, just before lunch Carleton himself strode into the room and said, 'You've had long enough.'

'Why, you lazy good-for-nothing brute!' Aunt Spiker shouted.
'Beat him!' cried Aunt Sponge.
'I certainly will!' Aunt Spiker snapped. She glared at James, and James looked back at her with large frightened eyes.
(James and the Giant Peach)

I am enclosing a time exposure of a bit of our study. You can see the paraphone in the far corner.

'Yes, Carleton,' the three of us murmured, trembling. We stood back, breathless from our exertions, compelled as always to wait and watch the dreadful Carleton while he performed the ritual of inspection. First of all, he would go to the drawer of his desk and take out a pure-white cotton glove which he slid with much ceremony on to his right hand. Then, taking as much care and time as a surgeon in an operating theatre, he would move slowly round the study, running his white-gloved fingers along all the ledges, along the tops of the picture-frames, over the surfaces of the desks, and even over the bars of the fire-grate. Every few seconds, he would hold those white fingers up close to his face, searching for traces of dust, and we three Fags would stand there watching him, hardly daring to breathe, waiting for the dreaded moment when the great man would stop and shout, 'Ha! What's this I see?' A look of triumph would light up his face as he held up a white finger which had on it the tiniest smudge of grey dust, and he would stare at us with his slightly popping pale blue eyes and say, 'You haven't cleaned it, have you? You haven't bothered to clean my study properly.'

To the three of us Fags who had been slaving away for the whole of the morning, these words were simply not true. 'We've cleaned every bit of it, Carleton,' we would answer. 'Every little bit.'

'In that case why has my finger got dust on it?' Carleton would say, tilting his head back and gazing at us down the length of his nose. 'This *is* dust, isn't it?'

We would step forward and peer at the white-gloved forefinger and at the tiny smidgin of dust that lay on it, and we would remain silent. I longed to point out to him that it was an actual impossibility to clean a much-used room to the point where no speck of dust remained, but that would have been suicide.

'Do any of you dispute the fact that this is dust?' Carleton would say, still holding up his finger. 'If I am wrong, do tell me.'

'It isn't *much* dust, Carleton.'

'I didn't ask you whether it was *much* dust or *not much* dust,' Carleton would say. 'I simply asked you whether or not it was dust. Might it, for example, be iron filings or face powder instead?'

'No, Carleton.'

'Or crushed diamonds, maybe?'

'No, Carleton.'

'Then what is it?'

'It's . . . it's dust, Carleton.'

'Thank you,' Carleton would say. 'At last you have admitted that you failed to clean my study properly. I shall therefore see all three of you in the changing-room tonight after prayers.'

> You seem to have been doing a lot of painting; but when you paint the lav. dont paint the seat, leaving it wet and sticky, or some unfortunate person who has not noticed it, will adhere to it, and when his bottom is cut off 'as she chooses' to go about with the seat sticking behind him always, he will be doomed to stay where he is

Roald Dahl was made 'Tip Fag' – whose job was to supervise the other Fags in Priory House – after only two terms at the school.

The rules and rituals of fagging at Repton were so complicated that I could fill a whole book with them. A House Boazer, for example, could make any Fag in the House do his bidding. He could stand anywhere he wanted to in the building, in the corridor, in the changing-room, in the yard, and yell 'Fa-a-ag!' at the top of his voice and every Fag in the place would have to drop what he was doing and run flat out to the source of the noise. There was always a mad stampede when the call of 'Fa-a-ag!' echoed through the House because the last boy to arrive would invariably be chosen for whatever menial or unpleasant task the Boazer had in mind.

During my first term, I was in the changing-room one day just before lunch scraping the mud from the soles of my studyholder's football boots when I heard the famous shout of 'Fa-a-ag!' far away at the other end of the House.

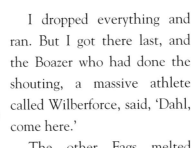

I dropped everything and ran. But I got there last, and the Boazer who had done the shouting, a massive athlete called Wilberforce, said, 'Dahl, come here.'

The other Fags melted away with the speed of light and I crept forward to receive my orders. 'Go and heat my seat in the bogs,' Wilberforce said. 'I want it *warm*.'

I hadn't the faintest idea what any of this meant, but I already knew better than to ask questions of a Boazer. I hurried away and found a fellow Fag who told me the meaning of this curious order. It meant that the Boazer wished to use lavatory but that he wanted the seat warmed for him before he sat down. The six House lavatories, none with doors, were situated in an unheated outhouse and on a cold day in winter you could get frostbite out there if you stayed too long. This particular day was icy-cold, and I went out through the snow into the outhouse and entered number one lavatory, which I knew was reserved for Boazers only. I wiped the frost off the seat with

The school-porter, Mr Pople, conducted an extraordinary ceremony at Repton . . .

'There were six lavatories in the school, numbered on their doors from one to six. Mr Pople, standing at the end of the long corridor, would have in the palm of his hand six small brass discs, each with a number on it, one to six. There was absolute silence as he allowed his eye to travel down the two lines of stiffly standing boys. Then he would bark out a name, "Arkle!" In this manner, six boys selected at Mr Pople's whim were dispatched to the lavatories to do their duty. Nobody asked them if they might or might not be ready to move their bowels at seven-thirty in the morning before breakfast. They were simply ordered to do so.'
(How I Became a Writer)

The Priory.
Repton.

Dear Mama,
Thanks for your post card. I
sent my Sunday letter off as usual.
Actually a fag of posted it, but he swears
he did so, because he went out
specially for the purpose.

As a **senior boy**, Roald Dahl **made use of Fags** himself, not to warm his loo seat but usually to **post** some of the many letters he wrote to his mother.

my handkerchief, then I lowered my trousers and sat down. I was there a full fifteen minutes in the freezing cold before Wilberforce arrived on the scene.

'Have you got the ice off it?' he asked.

'Yes, Wilberforce.'

'Is it *warm*?'

'It's as warm as I can get it, Wilberforce,' I said.

'We shall soon find out,' he said. 'You can get off now.'

I got off the lavatory seat and pulled up my trousers. Wilberforce lowered his own trousers and sat down. 'Very good,' he said. 'Very good indeed.' He was like a winetaster sampling an old claret. 'I shall put you on my list,' he added.

I stood there doing up my fly-buttons and not knowing what on earth he meant.

'Some Fags have cold bottoms,' he said, 'and some have hot ones. I only use hot-bottomed Fags to heat my bog-seat. I won't forget you.'

He didn't. From then on, all through that winter, I became Wilberforce's favourite bog-seat warmer, and I used always to keep a paperback book in the pocket of my tail-coat to while away the long bog-warming sessions. I must have read the entire works of Dickens sitting on that Boazer's bog during my first winter at Repton.

That Awful Cold Bath

Seniority (the number of terms you have been at school) was tremendously important. It was a crime for a boy to be 'sidey' (cheeky) to another boy who was a year or two senior to him. Once during my third year when I was sixteen, I was 'sidey' to a boy called W. W. Gregson who was seventeen. W. W. Gregson was a Studyholder. I wasn't but I was no longer a Fag. I was a Second, as they called it. W. W. Gregson didn't like me being 'sidey' to him, so he rounded up half-a-dozen other studyholders of his own age and they hunted me down. I ran into the yard where they cornered me and grabbed hold of my arms and legs and carried me bodily back into the 'house'. In the changing-room they held me down while one of them filled a bath brimful of icy cold water, and into this they dropped me, clothes and all and held me there for several agonising minutes.

"Push his head under!" cried W. W. Gregson. "That'll teach him to keep his mouth shut!" They pushed my head under many times, and I choked and spluttered and half-drowned, and when at last they released me and I crawled out of the bath, I didn't have any dry clothes to change into. But another Second of my age, whose name was Ashton, came to my rescue and produced a spare suit. I have been grateful to Ashton ever since for this act of mercy.

W. W. Gregson, my tormentor, came from the North Country and his family made snuff. Today one can still find the name Gregson on those little boxes of snuff they sell in tobacconists shops, even now, whenever I see one, I shiver and think of that awful cold bath.

Games and photography

It was always a surprise to me that I was good at games. It was an even greater surprise that I was exceptionally good at two of them. One of these was called fives, the other was squash-racquets.

Fives, which many of you will know nothing about, was taken seriously at Repton and we had a dozen massive glass-roofed fives courts kept always in perfect condition. We played the game of *Eton*-fives, which is always played by four people, two on each side, and basically it consists of hitting a small, hard, white, leather-covered ball with your gloved hands. The Americans have something like it which they call handball, but Eton-fives is far more complicated because the court has all manner of ledges and buttresses built into it which help to make it a subtle and crafty game.

Fives is possibly the fastest ball-game on earth, far faster than squash, and the little ball ricochets around the court at such a speed that sometimes you can hardly see it. You need a swift eye, strong wrists and a very quick pair of hands to play fives well, and it was a game I took to right from the beginning. You may find it hard to believe, but I became so good at it that I won both the junior and the senior school fives in the same year when I was fifteen. Soon I bore the splendid title 'Captain of Fives', and I would travel with my

'Eton-fives' was first played between the buttresses on the outside of the chapel at the famous public school, Eton College, which is where the 'ledges and buttresses' on the courts originated, and why the courts have only three walls instead of four. Players must hit the ball up on to the front wall of the court after no more than one bounce on the floor, though the ball can bounce any number of times on the ledges and buttresses!

Repton-fives courts, c.1933.

team to other schools like Shrewsbury and Uppingham to play matches. I loved it. It was a game without physical contact, and the quickness of the eye and the dancing of the feet were all that mattered.

A Captain of any game at Repton was an important person. He was the one who selected the members of the team for matches. He and only he could award 'colours' to others. He would award school 'colours' by walking up to the chosen boy after a match and shaking him by the hand and saying, 'Graggers on your teamer!' These were magic words. They entitled the new teamer to all manner of privileges including a different-coloured hat-band on his straw-hat and fancy braid around the edges of his blazer and different-coloured games clothes, and all sorts of other advertisements that made the teamer gloriously conspicuous among his fellows.

'Colours' are awards given to pupils or students who have excelled themselves in a sport.

Fives Team
Priory House

A Captain of any game, whether it was football, cricket, fives or squash, had many other duties. It was he who pinned the notice on the school notice-board on match days announcing the team. It was he who arranged fixtures by letter with other schools. It was he and only he who had it in his power to invite this master or that to play against him and his team on certain afternoons. All these responsibilities were given to me when I became Captain of Fives. Then came the snag. It was more or less taken for granted that a Captain would be made a Boazer in recognition of his talents – if not a School Boazer then certainly a House Boazer. But the authorities did not like me. I was not to be trusted. I did not like rules. I was unpredictable. I was therefore not Boazer material. There was no way they would agree to make me a House Boazer, let alone a School Boazer. Some people are born to wield power and to exercise authority. I was not one of them. I was in full agreement with my Housemaster when he explained this to me. I would have made a rotten Boazer. I would have let down the whole principle of Boazerdom by refusing to beat the Fags. I was probably the only Captain of any game who has never become a Boazer at Repton. I was certainly the only unBoazered Double Captain, because I was also Captain of squash-racquets. And to pile glory upon glory, I was in the school football team as well.

A boy who is good at games is usually treated with great civility by the masters at an English Public School. In much the same way, the ancient Greeks revered their athletes and made statues of them in marble. Athletes were the demigods, the chosen few. They could perform glamorous feats beyond the reach of ordinary mortals. Even

'bruised nose'

Postcard about winning
heavyweight boxing.

today, fine footballers and baseball players and runners and all other great sportsmen are much admired by the general public and advertisers use them to sell breakfast cereals. This never happened to me, and if you really want to know, I'm awfully glad it didn't.

But because I loved playing games, life for me at Repton was not totally without pleasure. Games-playing at school is always fun if you happen to be good at it, and it is hell if you are not. I was one of the lucky ones, and all those afternoons on the playing-fields and in the fives courts and in the squash courts made the otherwise grey and melancholy days pass a lot more quickly.

There was one other thing that gave me great pleasure at this school and that was photography. I was the only boy who practised it seriously, and it was not quite so simple a business fifty years ago as it is today. I made myself a little dark-room in a corner of the music building, and in there I loaded my glass plates and developed my negatives and enlarged them.

Arthur Norris,
the Arts Master.

Our Arts Master was a shy retiring man called Arthur Norris who kept himself well apart from the rest of the staff. Arthur Norris and I became close friends and during my last year he organized an exhibition of my photographs. He gave the whole of the Art School over to this project and helped me to get my enlargements framed. The exhibition was rather a success, and masters who had hardly ever spoken to me over the past four years would come up and say things like, 'It's quite extraordinary' . . . 'We didn't know we had an artist in our midst' . . . 'Are they for sale?'

Arthur Norris would give me tea and cakes in his flat and would talk to me about painters like Cézanne and Manet and Matisse, and I have a feeling that it was there, having tea with the gentle soft-spoken Mr Norris in his flat on Sunday

A **Zeiss** camera from the 1930s.

we won easily. I have been doing quite a lot of photographing lately. Here are some photographs. I have taken a lot out and given to the house photograph book. That one of the cow just after it has done puss has come out rather well. Those sheep are rather nice too. I had a devil of a job to get close to them, because they are so timid, and had to keep going ba-a-a the whole time!

'I have been doing quite a lot of photographing lately.'

This close-up **photograph** of plant tissue was taken by Roald Dahl in his final year at Repton. **He developed all his own photos too.**

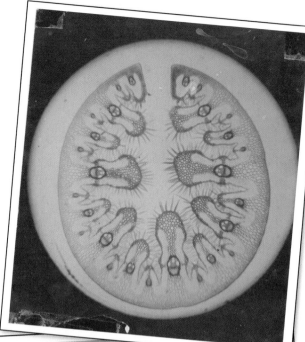

afternoons that my great love of painters and their work began.

After leaving school, I continued for a long time with photography and I became quite good at it. Today, given a 35mm camera and a built-in exposure-meter, anyone can be an expert photographer, but it was not so easy fifty years ago. I used glass plates instead of film, and each of these had to be loaded into its separate container in the dark-room before I set out to take pictures. I usually carried with me six loaded plates, which allowed me only six exposures, so that clicking the shutter even once was a serious business that had to be carefully thought out beforehand.

You may not believe it, but when I was eighteen I used to win prizes and medals from the Royal Photographic Society in London, and from other places like the Photographic Society of Holland. I even got a lovely big bronze medal from the Egyptian Photographic Society in Cairo, and I still have the photograph that won it. It is a picture of one of the so-called Seven Wonders of the World, the Arch of Ctesiphon in Iraq.

Ctesiphon was once the largest city in the world. Now all that remains is a ruined palace and the huge arch that Roald Dahl photographed during the Second World War. The Arch of Ctesiphon is 20 miles southeast of Baghdad in Iraq.

This is the largest unsupported arch on earth and I took the photograph while I was training out there for the RAF in 1940. I was flying over the desert solo in an old Hawker Hart biplane and I had my camera round my neck. When I spotted the huge arch standing alone in a sea of sand, I dropped one wing and hung in my straps and let go of the stick while I took aim and clicked the shutter. It came out fine.

Goodbye school

During my last year at Repton, my mother said to me, 'Would you like to go to Oxford or Cambridge when you leave school?' In those days it was not difficult to get into either of these great universities so long as you could pay.

'No, thank you,' I said. 'I want to go straight from school to work for a company that will send me to wonderful faraway places like Africa or China.'

You must remember that there was virtually no air travel in the early 1930s. Africa was two weeks away from England by boat and it took you about five weeks to get to China. These were distant and magic lands and nobody went to them just for a holiday. You went there to work. Nowadays you can go anywhere in the world in a few hours and nothing is fabulous any more. But it was a very different matter in 1934.

So during my last term I applied for a job only to those companies that would be sure to send me abroad. They were the Shell Company (Eastern Staff), Imperial Chemicals (Eastern Staff) and a Finnish lumber company whose name I have forgotten.

I was accepted by Imperial Chemicals and by the Finnish lumber company, but for some reason I wanted most of all to get into the Shell Company. When the day came for me to go up to London for this interview, my Housemaster told me it was ridiculous for me even to try. 'The Eastern Staff of Shell are the

In 1934, Shell's headquarters were at **Shell Mex House,** at 80 **Strand** in **London**. By a curious coincidence, this glamorous building is now the home of **Puffin**, Roald Dahl's publisher since 1973.

207

crème de la crème,' he said. 'There will be at least one hundred applicants and about five vacancies. Nobody has a hope unless he's been Head of the School or Head of the House, and you aren't even a *House* Prefect!'

My Housemaster was right about the applicants. There were one hundred and seven boys waiting to be interviewed when I arrived at the Head Office of the Shell Company in London. And there were seven places to be filled. Please don't ask me how I got one of those places. I don't know myself. But get it I did, and when I told my Housemaster the good news on my return to school, he didn't congratulate me or shake me warmly by the hand. He turned away muttering, 'All I can say is I'm damned glad I don't own any shares in Shell.'

I didn't care any longer what my Housemaster thought. I was all set. I had a career. It was lovely. I was to leave school for ever in July 1934 and join the Shell Company two months later in September when I would be exactly eighteen. I was to be an Eastern Staff Trainee at a salary of five pounds a week.

That summer, for the first time in my life, I did not accompany the family to Norway. I somehow felt the need for a special kind of last fling before I became a businessman. So while still at school during my last term, I signed up to spend August with something called 'The Public Schools' Exploring Society'. The leader of this outfit was a man who had gone with Captain Scott on his last expedition to the South Pole, and he was taking a party of senior schoolboys to explore the interior of Newfoundland during the summer holidays. It sounded like fun.

Without the slightest regret I said goodbye to Repton for ever and rode back to Kent on my motorbike. This splendid machine was a 500 cc Ariel which I had bought the year before for eighteen pounds, and during my last term at Repton

He might have remembered his new salary as being **five pounds a week**, but Roald Dahl was actually paid £2 1s 3d. But it was still an awful lot of money in 1934!

I kept it secretly in a garage along the Willington road about two miles away. On Sundays I used to walk to the garage and disguise myself in helmet, goggles, old raincoat and rubber waders and ride all over Derbyshire. It was fun to go roaring through Repton itself with nobody knowing who you were, swishing past the masters walking in the street and circling around the dangerous supercilious School Boazers out for their

An Ariel 500

got the job with Shell!

ALL COMMUNICATIONS TO BE ADDRESSED TO THE COMPANY.

TELEGRAPHIC ADDRESS:
"AUREOOL, LONDON."

TELEPHONE No.
AVENUE 8820.

THE ASIATIC PETROLEUM COMPANY, LIMITED.

ST HELENS COURT,
GREAT ST HELENS,
G.P.O. BOX 602.
LONDON, E.C.3.

ALL CODES USED.   DS

IN REPLY PLEASE REFER TO
G. S. E.   16th July, 1934.

Mr. R. Dahl,
    Repton School,
        Repton,
            Derbyshire.

Dear Sir,

With reference to our recent interview with you, we have now received a satisfactory report on your medical examination and are prepared to offer you a probationary position on our London Staff at a commencing salary of £130 per annum, with a view to your joining one of our foreign branches some time after you reach the age of 21, if your work and conduct in the London Office prove satisfactory, and you show such development during this probationary period as we expect from candidates whom we regard as suitable to be sent abroad in our foreign service.

In order that there may be no misunderstanding we place on record what was told you at the interview which we had with you - that in the event of your being required to take up a position on our foreign Staff outside Europe it

'if your work and conduct in the London Office prove satisfactory'

Sunday strolls. I tremble to think what would have happened to me had I been caught, but I wasn't caught. So on the last day of term I zoomed joyfully away and left school behind me for ever and ever. I was not quite eighteen.

I had only two days at home before I was off to Newfoundland with the Public Schools' Explorers. Our ship sailed from Liverpool at the beginning of August and took six

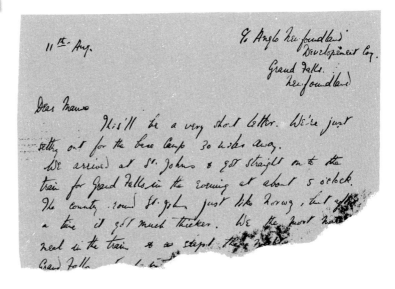

11th Aug.

To Anglo Newfoundland
Development Coy.
Grand Falls.
Newfoundland

Dear Mama

This'll be a very short letter. We're just setting out for the base camp 30 miles away. We arrived at St. Johns & got straight on to the train for Grand Falls in the evening at about 5 o'clock. The country round St. John just like Norway, but after a time it got much thicker. We the most near in the train so so slept. The Grand Falls

This is Roald Dahl's **passport**.

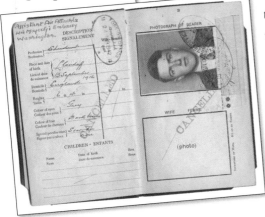

days to reach St John's. There were about thirty boys of my own age on the expedition as well as four experienced adult leaders. But Newfoundland, as I soon found out, was not much of a country. For three weeks we trudged all over that desolate land with enormous loads on our backs. We carried tents and groundsheets and sleeping-bags and saucepans and food and axes and everything else one needs in the interior of an unmapped, uninhabitable and inhospitable country. My own load, I know, weighed exactly one hundred and fourteen pounds, and someone else always had to help me hoist the rucksack on to my back in the mornings. We lived on pemmican and lentils, and the twelve of us who went separately on what was called the Long March from the north to the south of the island and back again suffered a good deal from lack of food. I can remember very clearly how we experimented with eating boiled lichen and reindeer moss to supplement our diet. But it *was* a genuine adventure and I returned home hard and fit and ready for anything.

There followed two years of intensive training with the Shell Company in England. We were seven trainees in that year's group and each one of us was being carefully prepared to uphold the majesty of the Shell Company in one or another remote tropical country. We spent weeks at the huge Shell Haven Refinery with a special instructor who taught us all about fuel oil and diesel oil and gas oil and lubricating oil and kerosene and gasoline.

After that we spent months at the Head Office in London learning how the great company functioned from the inside. I was still living in Bexley, Kent, with my mother and three sisters, and every morning, six days a week, Saturdays included, I would dress neatly in a sombre grey suit, have breakfast at seven forty-five and then, with a brown trilby on my head and a furled umbrella in my hand, I would board the eight-fifteen train to London together with a swarm of other equally sombre-suited businessmen. I found it easy to fall into their pattern. We were all very serious and dignified gents taking the train to our offices in the City of London where each of us, so we thought, was engaged in high finance and other enormously important

On board RMS *Nova Scotia*, 9th August: '. . . as Murray Levick said we were all to have our hair cut short I went along to Sam who cuts hair in his spare time (there is also a ship's barber) and had all my hair cut off! I've just got a tiny little bit of bristle on the top – I look fine.'

As ever, **Roald Dahl** wrote to his **mother** while he was away.
And he took plenty of photos too. Here are just a few of them.

11th. Aug.

To Anglo Newfoundland
Development Coy.
Grand Falls.
Newfoundland.

Dear Mama
This'll be a very short letter. We're just setting out for the base camp 30 miles away. We arrived at St. Johns & got straight on to the train for Grand Falls in the evening at about 5 o'clock.

'11th August:
Dear Mama,
This'll be a very short letter. We're just
setting out for the **base camp 30 miles away**.
We arrived at **St John's** and got straight on to
the train for **Grand Falls** in the evening at
about 5 o'clock . . .'

We are now right up in the north of Newfoundland & we are travelling due South & then South East about 80 miles. As I look south over Rattling Brook from here all I can see is pine clad hills & the none of the inhabitants have ever been

'. . . We are now right up in the **North** of Newfoundland
& we are travelling due **South** & then **South East** about
80 miles. As I look south over **Rattling Brook** from
here all I can see is pine-clad hills . . .'

Sleeping

Walking

Trekking

Eating

Daydreaming

matters. Most of my companions wore hard bowler hats, and a few like me wore soft trilbys, but not one of us on that train in the year of 1934 went bareheaded. It wasn't done. And none of us, even on the sunniest days, went without his furled umbrella. The umbrella was our badge of office. We felt naked without it. Also it was a sign of respectability. Road-menders and plumbers never went to work with umbrellas. Businessmen did.

When he worked for Shell, **Roald Dahl** used to buy a bar of Cadbury's Dairy Milk chocolate as a **lunchtime treat**. But he never threw away the silver paper. On his very first day, he rolled it into a tiny ball and left it on his desk. On the second day, he rolled the second bit of silver paper around the first. And so on. After a year, it was nearly as big as a **tennis ball**, and much, much **heavier**. When he was older, he kept the foil ball on a table beside his **writing chair**. It's still there.

the Businessman

I enjoyed it, I really did. I began to realize how simple life could be if one had a regular routine to follow with fixed hours and a fixed salary and very little original thinking to do. The life of a writer is absolute hell compared with the life of a businessman. The writer has to force himself to work. He has to make his own hours and if he doesn't go to his desk at all there is nobody to scold him. If he is a writer of fiction he lives in a world of fear. Each new day demands new ideas and he can never be sure whether he is going to come up with them or not. Two hours of writing fiction leaves this particular writer absolutely drained. For those two hours he has been miles away, he has been somewhere else, in a different place with totally different people, and the effort of swimming back into normal surroundings is very great. It is almost a shock. The writer walks out of his workroom in a daze. He wants a drink. He needs it. It happens to be a fact that nearly every writer of fiction in the world drinks more whisky than is good for him. He does it to give himself faith, hope and courage. A person is a fool to become a writer. His only compensation is absolute freedom. He has no master except his own soul, and that, I am sure, is why he does it.

The Shell Company did us proud. After twelve months at Head Office, we trainees were all sent away to various Shell branches in England to study salesmanship. I went to Somerset and spent several glorious weeks selling kerosene to old ladies in remote villages. My kerosene motor-tanker had a tap at the back and when I rolled into Shepton Mallet or Midsomer Norton or Peasedown St John or Hinton Blewett or Temple Cloud or Chew Magna or Huish Champflower, the old girls and the young maidens would hear the roar of my motor and would come out of their cottages with jugs and buckets to buy a gallon of kerosene for their lamps and their heaters. It is fun for a young man to do that sort of thing. Nobody gets a nervous breakdown or a heart attack from selling kerosene to gentle country folk from the back of a tanker in Somerset on a fine summer's day.

Then suddenly, in 1936, I was summoned back to Head Office in London. One of the Directors wished to see me. 'We are sending you to Egypt,' he said. 'It will be a three-year tour, then six months' leave. Be ready to go in one week's time.'

Roald Dahl never found writing easy. He wrote, rewrote and wrote again before he was satisfied with his stories. Much of his work went up in flames in the regular bonfires that he had outside his writing shed. Some of his books went through several incarnations, including this one. Two episodes of *Boy* first appeared in *The Witches*. *The BFG* first made an appearance in *Danny the Champion of the World*. And an early version of *Charlie and the Chocolate Factory* was once about a boy who was made entirely of chocolate! (*see page 183*)

'Oh, but sir!' I cried out. 'Not *Egypt*! I really don't want to go to *Egypt*!'

The great man reeled back in his chair as though I had slapped him in the face with a plate of poached eggs. 'Egypt,' he said slowly, 'is one of our finest and most important areas. We are doing you a *favour* in sending you there instead of to some mosquito-ridden place in the swamps!'

I kept silent.

'May I ask why you do not wish to go to Egypt?' he said.

I knew perfectly well why, but I didn't know how to put it. What I wanted was jungles and lions and elephants and tall coconut palms swaying on silvery beaches, and Egypt had none of that. Egypt was desert country. It was bare and sandy and full of tombs and relics and Egyptians and I didn't fancy it at all.

'What is wrong with Egypt?' the Director asked me again.

'It's . . . it's . . . it's,' I stammered, 'it's too *dusty*, sir.'

The man stared at me. 'Too *what?*' he cried.

'Dusty,' I said.

'*Dusty!*' he shouted. 'Too *dusty*! I've never heard such rubbish!'

There was a long silence. I was expecting him to tell me to fetch my hat and coat and leave the building for ever. But he didn't do that. He was an awfully nice man and his name was Mr Godber. He gave a deep sigh and rubbed a hand over his eyes and said, 'Very well then, if that's the way you want it. Redfearn will go to Egypt instead of you and you will have to take the next posting that comes up, dusty or not. Do you understand?'

'Yes, sir, I realize that.'

'If the next vacancy happens to be Siberia,' he said, 'you'll have to take it.'

'I quite understand, sir,' I said. 'And thank you very much.'

Within a week Mr Godber summoned me again to his office. 'You're going to East Africa,' he said.

'Hooray!' I shouted, jumping up and down. 'That's marvellous, sir! That's wonderful! How terrific!'

The great man smiled. 'It's quite dusty there too,' he said.

'Lions!' I cried. 'And elephants and giraffes and coconuts everywhere!'

'Your boat leaves from London Docks in six days,' he said. 'You get off at Mombasa. Your salary will be five hundred pounds per annum and your tour is for three years.'

I was twenty years old. I was off to East Africa where I would walk about in khaki shorts every day and wear a topi on my head! I was ecstatic. I rushed home and told my mother. 'And I'll be gone for three years,' I said.

I was her only son and we were very close. Most mothers, faced with a situation like this, would have shown a certain amount of distress. Three years is a long time and Africa was far away. There would be no visits in between. But my mother did not allow even the tiniest bit of what she must have felt to disturb my joy. 'Oh, well done you!' she cried. 'It's wonderful news! And it's just where you wanted to go, isn't it!'

The whole family came down to London Docks to see me off on the boat. It was a tremendous thing in those days for

Roald Dahl – in a **topi**, with a **coconut**! Now his **salary** was raised to **ten pounds a week**.

a young man to be going off to Africa to work. The journey alone would take two weeks, sailing through the Bay of Biscay, past Gibraltar, across the Mediterranean, through the Suez Canal and the Red Sea, calling in at Aden and arriving finally at Mombasa. What a prospect that was! I was off to the land of palm-trees and coconuts and coral reefs and lions and elephants and deadly snakes, and a white hunter who had lived ten years in Mwanza had told me that if a black mamba bit you, you died within the hour writhing in agony and foaming at the mouth. I couldn't wait.

Roald Dahl continued to write to his mother while he was away. And she kept every single one of his letters. They are now kept safely in the Roald Dahl Museum and Story Centre in Great Missenden.

Mama, 1936

Although I didn't know it at the time, I was sailing away for a good deal longer than three years because the Second World War was to come along in the middle of it all. But before that happened, I got my African adventure all right. I got the roasting heat and the crocodiles and the snakes and the long safaris up-country, selling Shell oil to the men who ran the diamond mines and the sisal plantations. I learned about an extraordinary machine called a decorticator (a name I have always loved) which shredded the big leathery sisal leaves into fibre. I learned to speak Swahili and to shake the scorpions out of my mosquito boots in the mornings. I learned what it was like to get malaria and to run a temperature of 105°F for three days, and when the rainy seasons came and the water poured down in solid sheets and flooded the little dirt roads, I learned how to spend nights in the back of a stifling station-wagon with all the windows closed against marauders from the jungle. Above all, I learned how to look after myself in a way that no young person can ever do by staying in civilization.

When the big war broke out in 1939, I was in Dar es Salaam, and from there I went up to Nairobi to join the RAF. Six months later, I was a fighter pilot flying Hurricanes all round the Mediterranean. I flew in the Western Desert of Libya, in Greece, in Palestine, in Syria, in Iraq and in Egypt. I shot down some German planes and I got shot down myself, crashing in a burst of flames and crawling out and getting rescued by brave soldiers crawling on their bellies over the sand. I spent six months in hospital in Alexandria, and when I came out, I flew again.

But all that is another story. It has nothing to do with childhood or school or Gobstoppers or dead mice or Boazers or summer holidays among the islands of Norway. It is a different tale altogether, and if all goes well, I may have a shot at telling it one of these days.

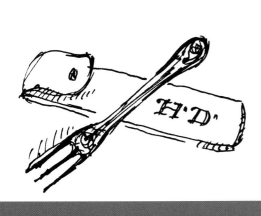

P.S.

Haifa, June 1941

The Voyage Out

The ship that was carrying me away from England to Africa in the autumn of 1938 was called the SS *Mantola*. She was an old paint-peeling tub of 9,000 tons with a single tall funnel and a vibrating engine that rattled the tea-cups in their saucers on the dining-room table.

The voyage from the Port of London to Mombasa would take two weeks and on the way we were going to call in at Marseilles, Malta, Port Said, Suez, Port Sudan and Aden. Nowadays you can fly to Mombasa in a few hours and you stop nowhere and nothing is fabulous any more, but in 1938 a journey like that was full of stepping-stones and East Africa was a long way from home, especially if your contract with the Shell Company said that you were to stay out there for three years at a stretch. I was twenty-two when I left. I would be twenty-five before I saw my family again.

This is the beginning of the next part of **Roald Dahl's** amazing adventure. You can read more about it in *Going Solo* . . .

A DAHL-TASTIC QUIZ

How big a **Roald Dahl fan** are you?
Take this **fiendishly difficult quiz** to find out . . .

If you get stuck, all of the answers can be found somewhere in *More About Boy*.

1. Roald Dahl's father lost his arm in a terrible accident, but he managed exceedingly well without it. What was the one thing that he found impossible to do?
    a. wash his hair
    b. cut the top off a soft boiled egg
    c. make a cup of tea

2. What was Roald's mother called?
    a. Sofie
    b. Astri
    c. Rosie

3. Where was Roald Dahl born?
    a. Oslo, Norway
    b. Leeds, England
    c. Llandaff, Wales

4. When Roald was very young, what were his favourite sweets?
    a. lemon drops and chocolate mice
    b. sherbet suckers and liquorice bootlaces
    c. Mars bars and Kit Kats

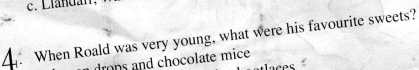

5. Whose blouse had toast-crumbs and tea stains and splotches of dried egg-yolk all over it?
    a. Mrs Pratchett, the owner of the sweet-shop
    b. Mrs Twit, the next door neighbour
    c. Mrs Smith, the vicar's wife

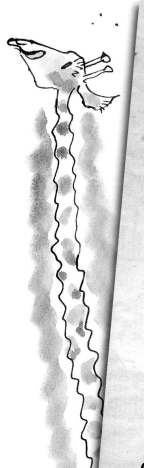

6. What's the Norwegian word for 'cheers'?
   a. tusen takk
   b. kringle
   c. skaal

7. Roald Dahl went to the same place on holiday every year from when he was four years old to when he was seventeen. Where was it?
   a. Norway
   b. Blackpool
   c. France

8. What is krokan?
   a. burnt toffee
   b. a monster
   c. a town in Norway

9. What was the "Hard Black Stinker"?
   a. a type of goat dropping
   b. a smelly Norwegian cheese
   c. a rickety old boat

10. What was the name of Roald Dahl's first boarding school?
   a. St. Paul's
   b. St. Peter's
   c. St. Michael's

11. According to Matron, what disgusting habit was only done by the lower classes?
    a. farting
    b. nose-picking
    c. snoring

12. What did Roald nearly lose in a car accident?
    a. his nose
    b. his driving licence
    c. his wallet

13. What colour was Captain Hardcastle's moustache?
    a. black
    b. orange
    c. green

14. What was the very worst punishment at the schools Roald Dahl attended?
    a. the cane
    b. the whip
    c. the chokey

15. What were Boazers?
    a. dinner ladies
    b. prefects
    c. French teachers

16. Who was Roald Dahl's first employer?
a. the Shell Company
b. British Gas
c. General Electric

17. What is a topi?
a. a belt
b. a coat
c. a hat

18. Name one of the Seven Wonders of the World.
a) the Arch of Ctesiphon
b) the Pillar of Plato
c) the Bridge of Sighs

19. How old was Roald Dahl when he went to live in Africa?
a) 5
b) 20
c) 32

20. What kind of plane did Roald Dahl fly in the war?
a. a Typhoon
b. a Spitfire
c. a Hurricane

ANSWERS

1. b) cut the top off a soft boiled egg.

2. a) Sofie.

3. c) Llandaff, Wales.

4. b) sherbet suckers and liquorice bootlaces.

5. a) Mrs Pratchett, the owner of the sweet-shop

6. c) skaal.

7. a) Norway.

8. a) burnt toffee.

9. c) a rickety old boat.

10. b) St. Peter's.

11. c) snoring.

12. a) his nose.

13. b) orange.

14. a) the cane.

15. b) prefects.

16. a) the Shell Company.

17. c) a hat.

18. a) the Arch of Ctesiphon.

19. b) 20.

20. a) Hurricane.

STORIES ARE GOOD FOR YOU.

Roald Dahl said,
*'If you have good thoughts, they will shine
out of your face like sunbeams and you
will always look lovely.'*

We believe in doing good things.
That's why ten per cent of all Roald Dahl income*
goes to our charity partners. We have supported
causes including: specialist children's nurses, grants for
families in need, and educational outreach programmes.
Thank you for helping us to sustain this vital work.

Find out more at roalddahl.com

Love from
BOY